The Daughters of the Republic of Texas
District VIII

Presents

Seconds of
A Pinch of This
and a
Handful of That

1830–1900

EAKIN PRESS ★ Austin, Texas

DISCLAIMER

The home remedies and household hints contained in this book are provided for historical purposes only. No express or implied warranties with regard to their efficacy or safety are made by the Daughters of the Republic of Texas, District VIII. Do not use them without first consulting a physician or other appropriate medical professional. Daughters of the Republic of Texas are not engaged in rendering medical advice.

FIRST EDITION

Copyright © 1994
By the Daughters of the Republic of Texas
District VIII

Published in the United States of America
By Eakin Press
An Imprint of Sunbelt Media, Inc., P.O. Drawer 90159
Austin, Texas 78709

ALL RIGHTS RESERVED. No part of this book may be reproduced in any form without written permission from the publisher, except for brief passages included in a review appearing in a newspaper or magazine.

ISBN 0-89015-970-X

Library of Congress Cataloging-in-Publication Data

Seconds of a pinch of this and a handful of that, 1830–1900 / The Daughters of the Republic of Texas, District VIII.
   p. cm.
Includes bibliographical references and index.
   1. Cookery. 2. Cookery — Texas. 3. Texas — Social life and customs. I. Daughters of the Republic of Texas. District VIII.
TX714.S44   1944
641.5 — dc20   93-48249
                                                                                  CIP

*This book is dedicated
to the memory of all pioneer women
and the memory of*
*Delma Thames, Editor
and
Ellagene Stenger, Member of the Publishing Committee
of the first volume of DRT District VIII's,*
A Pinch of This and a Handful of That.

Contents

Acknowledgments	vi
Foreword	vii
Preface	ix
Options at Sea	1
Beverages	9
Breads	13
Soups	26
Butter, Cheese, and Eggs	31
Fish	36
Meat, Poultry, and Game	41
Sauces and Dressings	56
Dumplings	60
Salads and Salad Dressing	62
Vegetables and Pasta	69
Cakes	79
Cookies	96
Puddings	103
Pastry, Pies, and Tarts	109
Custards, Creams, and Desserts	122
Candy	132
Canning and Pickling	140
Household Hints	148
Home Remedies	168
Conversion Charts	179
Translations	182
Contributors	183
Bibliography	201
Index	203

Acknowledgments

PUBLISHING COMMITTEE

Frances Brady Underwood,
  Chairman
Caroline Boales Bass,
  Recording Secretary
Luciclaire Rankin Proud,
  Treasurer
Jan Felts Bullock
Myrtle Hornsby Callan
Jeanette Streuer Felger
Alyce Boscamp Ferguson
Linda Hurt Halliburton

Lel Purcell Hawkins
Katheryn Nagel Kiser
Betty McCarty McAnelly
Billie Merkle McMullen
Marie Streuer Offerman
Clara Reed Parr
Crystal Sasse Ragsdale
Michelle Robertson
Lillian Fietsam Stuesser
Carolyn Garner Thurmond

The Daughters of the Republic of Texas, District VIII, wish to thank all individuals who donated their favorite ancestor recipes and helpful hints, and to those who helped with the compiling and the selling or in any other way contributed to the publication of this historic book.

Foreword

After reading this remarkable book, I knew instantly why the Daughters of the Republic of Texas asked me to write the foreword. I am a Texas artifact. Through seven decades of living I have witnessed a lot of Texas history and, like many daughters and great, great-granddaughters of pioneer Texas, thrilled to the fact that women have been a vital part of its history.

Long before it was a state, Texas women made this cantankerous land livable and lovable. From the very beginning gentle women like the Indian maiden, Angelina, guided explorers as they arrived on the Texas Gulf Coast. Women were inside the besieged Alamo and on the bayous of San Jacinto. Women stood on the farm and at the front of schoolrooms. I love the story of the seven French nuns who arrived in San Antonio at the Ursiline Convent which became an academy of learning—something that looked like a hopeless task.

One sister wrote home, "Great allowances must be made for people growing up in this country (Texas had just been a state for six years). It is scarcely possible for them to advance to the same degree of perfection as those from the old country— the devil having had full sway here for so many years, he still exercises considerable influence over souls." And we're still fighting it today.

Whether in the cities or on the plains, women built this state in and outside the kitchen. Mary Ann Goodnight, a lonely West Texas ranchwoman, welcomed traveling cowboys to her table. One guest left her two chickens for Sunday dinner. She made pets of them and wrote her sister, "No one knows what company a couple of chickens can be."

Seconds of A Pinch of This and a Handful of That tells the story of women like these through recipes handed down generation to generation. From Mrs. Ten Evck's Molasses Pie and Oxmarrow-Pomade for the Hair to advice on caring for an infant and making a happy marriage, these ancestors had a recipe for everything they faced.

Their story is a story of can-do spirit of grit and love handed down along with their recipes to their daughters. It is still strong in all Texas women and prodding us on to new frontiers.

— LIZ CARPENTER

Preface

The Daughters of the Republic of Texas, District VIII, have collected for this book additional recipes, household hints, and home remedies dating from the days of the Republic to the turn of the century.

Family names appear with the recipe when the material is known to have passed through the family for generations to the present time. Where a year appears with the recipe, the item is known to have been in use at that time. It is our desire for this book to present a concept of a way of life. The many roles of the pioneer women are portrayed in this book as wife, mother, housekeeper, and doctor/nurse as well as that of artist and writer. Early Texas history is woefully lacking in knowledge of the role women played in the development of Texas.

Some of the original spelling, grammar, and format of the recipes, household hints, and home remedies are retained in this book so that the flavor, customs, and usages of the period would not be lost.

The Daughters of the Republic of Texas, District VIII, is part of a ten district area of Texas. Members are descended from soldiers, sailors, and citizens of the Republic of Texas who resided in Texas prior to February 19, 1846. Many of their ancestors fought for the independence of Texas at famous battles such as the Alamo, San Jacinto, and the Siege of Bexar.

The funds generated from the sale of this book will go toward a statue to be placed on the state of Texas Capitol grounds. This statue will be a memorial to all pioneer women of Texas and will be the first memorial statue of a woman to be placed on the grounds of the Capitol.

DAUGHTERS OF THE REPUBLIC OF TEXAS

OUR ASSOCIATION

The Daughters of the Lone Star Republic was organized by cousins Betty Ballinger and Hally Bryan.

They conceived the idea in 1891 of perpetuating forever the memory of the Texas pioneer families and soldiers of the Republic of Texas by forming an association of their descendants. This organization would soon come to be known as the Daughters of the Republic of Texas.

OBJECTIVES

1. To perpetuate the memory and spirit of the men and women who achieved and maintained the independence of Texas.

2. To encourage historical research into the earliest records of Texas, especially those relating to the Revolution of 1835 and the events which followed; to foster the preservation of documents and relics; to encourage the publication of records of the individual service of the soldiers and patriots of the Republic, and other source material for the history of Texas.

3. To promote the celebration of Texas Honor Days: Lamar Day, January 26; Texas Statehood Day, February 19; Texas Independence Day, and Flag Day, March 2; Alamo Heroes Day, March 6; San Jacinto Day, April 21; Gonzales Day, October 2; Stephen F. Austin's Birthday, November 3; and Founders Day, November 6.

4. To memorialize all historic spots by erecting markers thereon; and to cherish and preserve the unity of Texas as achieved and established by the fathers and mothers of the Texas Revolution.

THE ALAMO

Travis, Bowie, Crockett, Bonham are names forever connected with the heroic cause of liberty. These dedicated men and 185 others, fought more than four thousand Mexican troops led by Santa Anna during a thirteen day siege.

The defeat of the Alamo was the rallying point in the Texas Revolution. "Remember the Alamo!" was the cry as Texans fought for freedom from tyranny and for a government separate from that of Mexico.

Erected in 1754, the Alamo was used as a chapel for the Mission San Antonio de Valero. Occupied and abandoned many times over the years, it was in disrepair by the early 1900s.

Miss Clara Driscoll purchased property north of the Chapel in 1903 when the Daughters learned the site was to be sold for a hotel. The state reimbursed her in 1905 and turned the Alamo over to the care of the Daughters.

Location: Corner of Houston and Alamo streets, San Antonio
Hours: 9 A.M. to 5:30 P.M., Monday through Saturday; 10:00 A.M. to 5:30 P.M. Sunday. Closed December 24 and 25 and for special occasions.
Admission: None — Donations accepted
Address: P.O. Box 2599, San Antonio, TX 78299
Telephone: (210) 225-1391

FRENCH LEGATION

Construction of the French Legation began in 1840 and was completed in the spring of 1841. The Legation was built by Comte Alphonse Dubois de Saligny, Charge d' Affaires of his Majesty Louis Philippe, King of France, to the Republic of Texas. The house was purchased in 1948 by the State of Texas from the Robertsons, who owned and lived in the Legation for 100 years. The historic house was put into the custody of the Daughters of the Republic of Texas by the state in 1949. The Daughters have restored and maintained the Legation for the public to whom it was opened as a museum on April 5, 1956.

Location: 802 San Marcos Street, Austin, TX
Hours: 1 P.M. to 5 P.M.; closed Sunday and Monday
Admission: $2.50 adults and $1.00 for Children
Address: 802 San Marcos St., Austin, TX 78702
Telephone: (512) 472-8189

DRT HEADQUARTERS AND REPUBLIC OF TEXAS MUSEUM

The **Republic of Texas Museum** was housed, in 1903, in one room of the state Capitol building. The collection of Republic era artifacts grew rapidly through the dedicated efforts of the DRT and more space was required.

The Land Department moved in 1916 from the Old Land Office building on the Capitol grounds and a portion of the structure was turned over to the Daughters of the Republic of Texas for use as a museum.

The DRT museum occupied the second floor of the building until 1989 when restoration of the deteriorating structure began. Four years later, during the 100th year of the DRT, the Daughters purchased a building of their own to house the museum and the organization's headquarters.

The **Business Office,** located in the west portion of the building, handles the sale of many DRT related items, including stationery, the annual publication, the Manual of Procedure, and all books published by the DRT.

The office also maintains the membership records of the association and houses all of the applications and related documents from 1891 to the present. The office staff can do limited searches on ancestors registered with the DRT for a small fee plus copying costs.

Location: 510 East Anderson Lane, Austin, TX
Hours: *Business Office,* 8 A.M. to 5 P.M., Monday through Friday; *Republic of Texas Museum,* 1 September–31 May, 11 A.M. to 4 P.M., Monday through Friday; 1 June–31 August, 11 A.M. to 4 P.M., Tuesday through Saturday
Admission: Adults, $2.00; Children, 50 cents; and DRT Members, $1.00
Address: 510 East Anderson Lane (It is also Hwy. 183 — the museum is ½ blk. west of I.H. 35 North.), Austin, TX 78752
Phone: (512) 339-1997

THE CRADLE

This building was originally the law office of William Pitt Ballinger, father of co-founder Betty Ballinger. Now known as the Cradle, it is cherished by the Daughters as the place where Miss Ballanger and her first cousin Hally Bryan Perry formulated the idea for their new organization. The Cradle has recently been restored to reflect the original furnishings of the late 1800s.
Location: 2903 Ave. O½, Galveston
Hours: By Appointment
Admission: None—Donations Accepted
Address: P.O. Box 3537, Galveston, TX 77552

DRT LIBRARY

The Texas History Research Library is part of the Alamo complex and has been developed and is supported and maintained by the DRT for the use of all researchers.

The need to encourage the study of Texas history and to preserve its documents was of sufficient importance to the founders of the DRT to be stipulated specifically in their charter, in 1893.

The library contains materials pertaining to the history of Texas in particular, the period of the Texas Republic and associated fields. Books, documents, maps, photographs, periodicals, early newspapers, clippings, and family papers are among the materials in the library's files and closed stacks.

A card catalog is available for the use of researchers to locate information, and library attendants provide assistance in retrieving materials for use. Duplication services and photographic reproduction services are available.

Options at Sea

This section contains recipes of the foods the Germans immigrating to Texas were served while at sea. These recipes have been researched from old German cookbooks and updated to modern measurements.   *Marie Offerman*

Sunday
Plum Soup
½ lb. beef
Meal Pudding

Monday
Pea Soup
½ lb. beef
Thick rice with syrup

Tuesday
Barley Soup
½ lb. beef
Lentils or beans as vegetables

Wednesday
Navy Bean Soup
½ lb. beef
Sauerkraut or green beans

Thursday
Plum Soup
½ lb. beef
Meal Pudding

Friday
Pea soup
½ lb. beef
Sauerkraut or green beans

Saturday
Green pea soup
½ lb. beef
Lentils or beans as vegetables

Weekly Rations for Each Adult	Further for Each Adult
4 oz. coffee	1½ hogshead drinking water
2 oz. tea	for voyage to Texas
8 oz. sugar	30–40 lbs. of potatoes
16 oz. butter	according to season
5 lb. bread	Salt, Mustard, Pepper
¼ bottle of wine	Vinegar, medicines

– Sophienburg Museum, New Braunfels, TX

PFLAUMEN SUPPE

(Plum Soup)

1½ lbs. fresh plums	1 tbsp. lemon juice
1 liter water (4½ cups)	½ cup white wine
Lemon rind from 1 lemon (only the yellow part)	(or apple cider, if wine is not available)
1½ tbsp. cornstarch or 2 tbsp. Tapioca	Buttered toasted small bread cubes
3 tbsp. water	3 tbsp. butter, melted
¼ tsp. cinnamon	Granulated sugar to sprinkle on bread cubes, optional
¼ cup sugar	
Dash of ground cloves, optional	

Wash the fruit, remove seeds and slice the fruit. Place in a 3-qt. pan; add the water and lemon rind and simmer until tender. Rub the fruit through a food mill or sieve. Return the sieved fruit to the saucepan and bring to a boil; remove from the heat and stir in the cornstarch that has been mixed with the 3 tbsp. of water. Continue stirring and bring to a boil again. Cook gently until done, stirring frequently, about 5 to 10 minutes (a little longer for tapioca). Season with cinnamon, sugar, cloves, lemon juice and wine to your taste. *Note:* Tart fruit may require more sugar.

   Serve hot or cold. Just before serving sprinkle top with the toasted bread cubes. To make bread cubes: cut bread in small cubes (1 cup) and toast by placing in a moderate oven until cubes are dry. Add butter and stir the cubes until they are well coated. Add more butter if necessary. Return to oven and toast until golden. Sprinkle with a little granulated sugar, if desired. Cool and store in a sealed container. Sprinkle on soup just before serving. Other fruits, such as apples, pears or cherries may be substituted for the plums; or a mixture of fruit may be used.

DICKER REISBREI MIT MELASSES, ZUCKERSYRUP ODER HONIG SUSSER DICKER REISBREL

(Sweet Thick Rice)

On board ship Dicker Reisbrei *was served with* melasses *(molasses),* zuckersyrup *(sugar syrup) or* honig *(honey). The rice would have been cooked in salt water (probably sea water) until very thick and then served with the available syrup. This was one of the few sweet dishes served aboard ship. Water was very precious and I'm sure they tried to collect as much rainwater as possible, and then used it sparingly.*

When the immigrants arrived in Texas and became established in their new homes, they were able to make Susser Dicker Reisbrei *(Sweet Thick Rice) as they had been accustomed to in Germany. There are many versions of Sweet Thick Rice, but basically they are all creamed rice dishes, sweetened with sugar and flavored with cinnamon and butter.*

SWEET THICK RICE

1 cup raw plain rice
2 cups boiling water
1 tsp. salt
3 to 4 cups milk

¼ cup sugar or more to taste
1 to 3 tsp. cinnamon
¼ cup butter

In a saucepan, add rice, salt and a little butter (1 tbsp.) to boiling water. Reduce heat and simmer covered about 20 minutes or until most of the water is absorbed. Add milk and simmer, uncovered until the rice is tender and mixture is creamy and thick, not soupy. Stir frequently to prevent sticking and scorching. Add more milk, if needed. Some people prefer to add the sugar with the milk and others sprinkle the sugar on top. When rice is done, put in an oven proof dish. Brown the butter lightly and pour over rice and sprinkle generously with sugar and cinnamon. Keep rice warm until ready to serve. Rice may be served cold, but my preference is warm. Sweet rice is served with the main meal.

There are many variations in old German cookbooks. Several added a little grated lemon rind, or served the rice with a wine sauce or syrups, such as molasses or honey. In some recipes a cinnamon stick was cooked with the rice until ready to serve, then removed and cinnamon was sprinkled lightly on top with sugar. If the rice is served cold, allowance must be made for extra thickening as it cools. The butter would be cooked with the rice, using only 1 to 2 tbsp. and omitting the butter on top and sprinkling with sugar and cinnamon while rice is still warm.

MEAL PUDDING
Really Mehl (Flour) Pudding

The journey to Texas for the immigrants from Germany took about two months. Ships carried provisions for ninety days in case of delays due to storms or calm seas, since sailing vessels were used at the time. The food served on board ship was rather monotonous. Food preservation methods were inadequate and space was limited, so menus were repeated several times a week. The recipe for Mehl (flour) Pudding is a more modern version, but basically the same that would have been made on board ship or in homes that were established here.

MEHL (FLOUR) PUDDING

¾ cup butter or margarine
1 quart milk, scalded
9 eggs, separated

¾ cup flour
1 cup sugar
1 tsp. vanilla (optional)

Soften the butter and blend well with the flour until smooth. Add the sugar and milk, and pour the mixture into the top of a double boiler and cook until slightly thickened and creamy.

Stir frequently to prevent lumping. Cool the mixture to luke warm add egg yolks, one at a time, beating well after each addition. *Modern note:* Pour the milk mixture into the large electric mixer bowl, when mixture is lukewarm add eggs and beat well. Add the vanilla if desired and then beat the egg whites until stiff and fold into pudding mixture. Grease 2 glass baking pans (7½ x 11½ in.) and slowly pour mixture into pans. Bake in slow oven for one hour. *Note:* The pudding will puff up and then fall. It is best not to open the oven door during baking. Makes 12 to 14 servings. Serve pudding with wine sauce or fruit.

Variation: The pudding is also made with yeast, using less eggs. This variation takes much longer to cook. Some recipes also added raisins or lemon peel. One recipe suggested serving the pudding with roast and stewed fruit. Rum sauce was also suggested. Nutmeg could be added if desired. A little salt was added to some recipes.

WEIN (WINE) BEIGUSS (SAUCE) FOR PUDDING

⅔ cup sugar
1½ cups water
Grated lemon rind to taste

2 tbsp. cornstarch
1 cup or little more sweet wine

Combine the sugar and cornstarch in a saucepan and mix well. Stir in cold water. Cook over low heat and stir constantly until mixture is clear. Remove from heat and add wine and lemon rind. Serve over hot pudding.

BOILED PORK

(gekochtes Schweinefleisch)

3 lbs. port (ribs, shoulder, etc.
 — skin may be left on)
Salt
3 quarts water

1 carrot
1 leek of small onion
1 stalk celery

Wash the meat and dry. Bring the water and desired amount of salt to a boil. Add the meat and vegetables bring back to a boil. Lower the heat to keep the meat simmering about 2 hours. Check for tenderness. When done, remove from heat and let sit in broth until ready to serve, about 10 to 20 minutes. Slice if necessary. *Note:* The broth may be used to make pannas (scrapple). Serve with boiled potatoes or dumplings, mustard, sauerkraut and sliced onions.

WHITE BREAD

6 pkgs. dry yeast
½ cup sugar

2 cups warm water
(105–114 degrees)

In a large mixing bowl combine sugar and water, stir to dissolve sugar, add the yeast, stir and let rise 5 to 10 minutes to proof yeast, and yeast dissolves. Add:

3 tbsp. corn oil
2 cups warm water

2 tbsp. salt

Stir well and add enough flour to make a stiff dough. Place dough on floured board and knead well, about 10 minutes. Place dough in a greased bowl and let rise until double in bulk; punch down and let rise again until doubled. Divide dough into 4 equal parts and roll into oblong loaves. Place on greased large cookie sheets. Cut diagonal slits in the tops with a sharp knife. Let rise until double. Bake in a 350-degree oven for 45 minutes. Remove from oven and brush with 1 egg beaten with a little water. Return to oven and bake 15 minutes more. For a very hard crust bake bread with a pan of water in bottom of oven. Keeps well and freezes. Excellent for sausage sandwiches, as well as other sandwiches and toast. (Six packages of yeast is correct.)

LENTIL SOUP (LINSEN SUPPE)

Soups have always been a favorite and thrifty dish for German people. The rations at sea, on the voyage to the United States, included many soups. Lentils were used in soup and also as vegetables. To this day lentil soup is a favorite in New Braunfels, especially to the descendants of the early settlers.

1 lb. dried lentils, washed and foreign objects removed	¼ tsp. pepper
2 to 3 quarts water	1 ham bone or shank, pork ribs, or smoked or salted ribs, or smoked pork chops or sausage
¼ cup diced salt pork or bacon	
¾ cup chopped onion	
¾ cup finely chopped carrots	2 tbsp. minced parsley (fresh or 1 tablespoon dry)
¾ cup finely chopped celery or celery root	
1 cup finely diced potatoes	Butter and flour to thicken, if desired
1 clove garlic, minced	A little vinegar, to taste, if desired
1 bay leaf	
1½ tsp. salt	Spaetzle

Soak dried lentils in cold water overnight. The next day, put in soup kettle, using soaking water. Start simmering while preparing the salt pork and vegetables. Cook salt pork or bacon in a skillet for about 5 minutes; add the onion, carrots, celery, potatoes and garlic. Simmer slowly about 10 minutes until the vegetables are softened, but not browned. Add mixture to the lentils. Add seasonings and ham bone or shank. Bring to a boil; reduce heat and simmer gently about 2 hours. Remove bones and any meat. Cut meat in bite size pieces. Press vegetables through a sieve, or blend. This will help thicken the soup. It is not necessary to sieve all the soup. *Note:* If sausage is used, parboil about ten minutes to remove some of the fat. Slice or cut in small pieces and simmer in the soup for a few minutes after it is sieved. Add the meat from the ham. If thicker soup is desired, mix a little butter and flour and add to soup. Stir well. Make the spaetzle and cook in soup before thickening or cook spaetzle in broth or water in a separate kettle and add to soup. Season soup with a little vinegar, if desired and garnish with parsley or put some in the soup. If the spaetzle are cooked in the soup, it will help thicken the soup a little. This soup is really a complete meal. Serve with homemade bread and butter. Serves 8.

SPAETZLE

1 egg per person
1 tbsp. lukewarm water
Pinch of salt

Flour to make a firm dough, but not too stiff
Broth or water

Beat the egg, water and salt together. Add enough flour to make a firm dough. Let dough rest about 15 minutes. Then put dough in a spaetzle press that has been dipped in water. Press the spaetzle into boiling broth or boiling salted water. A spaghetti cooker works well. Cook about a minute or two until spaetzle rise to the top. Lift spaetzel out of water and put in another pot with melted butter. Stir to lightly coat spaetzle. Keep warm until ready to serve — keeping on very low heat. Serve with gravy or browned butter with browned bread crumbs. If desired, cook spaetzle in soup, using 1 egg portion for 2 servings. If a spaetzle machine is not available, the dough can be dropped into the soup in small teaspoonfuls or roll the dough in small rolls and cut quickly and drop into the soup.

(These recipes were featured at the 1988, 1989, 1990, 1991, and 1992 Christmas Candlelight Tours in New Braunfels, Texas.)

Beverages

WEINSAFT (GRAPE JUICE)

5 lbs. ripe grapes, washed   1 qt. water
1 lb sugar, amount depends on the sweetness of the grapes

Cook washed grapes and water together for 5 to 10 minutes and strain through a muslin cloth. Squeeze hard to extract as much juice as possible. Add sugar and taste test for sweetness. Cook juice and sugar mixture for 15 minutes. Fill hot sterilized bottles and seal. (*Concord or very ripe Mustang grapes make a pretty colored juice. Wanda Nowotny Streuer, would mix 1 qt. grape juice with 1 qt. of lemonade for her special drink she called "Pretty Juice."*)

GERMAN CHAMPAGNE PUNCH

1 pint fresh sliced peaches, sugared lightly to draw juice
2 qts. white Rhine wine
1 pint fresh strawberries
2 liters ginger ale
$\frac{1}{5}$ champagne

Combine the peaches and wine several hours before serving. (This improves the flavor, but this step may be omitted if time is short.) Chill all ingredients. When ready to serve, pour the wine and peach mixture in the punch bowl and add the champagne and ginger ale. Do not add ice. Garnish with fresh strawberries, if desired. Makes about 24 servings.

CHERRY BRANDY

Cherries: 36 lbs., half red and half black; squeeze them with the hands, and add 1½ gallons of brandy. Let them infuse 24 hours; then put the bruised cherries and liquor into a canvas bag, a little at a time, and press it as long as it will run. Sweeten with fine sugar, and let it stand a month; bottle off, putting loaf sugar into every bottle.

CURRANT OR BLACKBERRY WINE
Mrs. G. A. Searight, 1891

One qt. of juice, two qts. of water, three lbs. of sugar, will make one gallon of wine. Put in jug, and as it ferments keep it filled with juice or sweetened water, and do not cork until after fermenting. Turn a cup over the top.

BLACKBERRY CORDIAL
Mrs. W. M. Walton, 1891

Take the ripest berries; mash them, put them in a linen bag and squeeze out the juice. To every quart of juice allow a pound of white sugar. Put the sugar into a large preserving kettle, pour the juice on it. When it is all melted, set it on the fire and boil it to a thin jelly. When cold, to every quart of juice allow a quart of brandy. Stir them well together and bottle for use. It will be ready at once.

QUINCE CORDIAL
Mrs. G. A. Searight, 1891

Grate quinces and squeeze the juice out through a cloth. To one qt. of juice take two qts. of water, three lbs. of sugar, one qt. of rum. Ready for use as soon as made.

HOW TO MAKE COFFEE
Mrs. J. L. Driskill, 1891

Take one pint of ground coffee and mix well with the white of an egg and enough cold water to thoroughly moisten it. Place in a well scalded coffee boiler and pour in one gallon of boiling water. Boil rather fast for five minutes, stirring down from the top and sides as it boils up, and place on back of the stove or range, where it will only simmer for ten or fifteen minutes longer. When ready to serve add a little more boiling water.

CREAM SODA WITHOUT A FOUNTAIN
1898

Coffee sugar, 4 lbs.; water, 3 pints; nutmegs, grated, 3 in number; whites of 10 eggs, well beaten; gum arabic, 1 oz.; oil of lemon, 20 drops, or extract equal to that amount. By using oils of other fruits you can make as many flavors from this as you desire, or prefer. Mix all and place over a gentle fire, and stir well about thirty minutes; remove from the fire, strain, and divide into two parts; into one-half put super-carbonate of soda, eight oz.; and into the other half put six oz. tartaric acid; shake well, and when cold they are ready to use, by pouring three or four spoons, from both parts, into separate glasses which are one-third full of cool water; stir each and pour together, and you have as nice a glass of cream soda as was ever drank, which can also be drank at your leisure, as the gum and eggs hold the gas.

AROMATIC BEER
1898

For 3 gals. water put in 1 qt. and ½ pint of molasses, 3 eggs well beaten, yeast, 1 gill. Into 2 qts. of the water, boiling hot, put 50 drops of oil you wish the flavor of; or mix 1 oz. each, oils sassafras, spruce and wintergreen, then use 50 drops of mixed oils. Mix all and strain; let it stand two hours, then bottle, bearing in mind that yeast must not be put in when the fluid would scald the hand. Boiling water cuts oil for beers, equal to alcohol.

A TEMPERANCE PLEDGE
1887

A pledge I make, no wine to take;
Nor brandy red, that turns the head;
Nor whisky hot, that makes the sot;
Nor fiery rum, that ruins the home;
Nor will I sin, by drinking gin;
Hard cider, too, will never do;
Nor lager beer, my heart to cheer;
Nor sparkling ale, my face to pale;
To quench my thirst I'll always bring,
Cold water from the well or spring;
So here I pledge perpetual hate,
To all that can intoxicate.

Breads

APPLE FRITTERS
From Grandma's Cookbook

Peel apples, and take out the core, cut the apples in thick slices, crosswise—this makes a ring. Sprinkle with sugar and let them lie for an hour, then dip each piece in batter, and fry until of a light brown color. Sprinkle again with sugar and send to the table.

BATTER FOR FRITTERS: Use 2 cups of flour and 2 eggs. Beat the eggs and flour together, and add enough sweet milk to make a batter of the consistency of griddle cakes; then beat in a level teaspoon of salt. This batter is simply made, and can be used for any kind of fritters.

BAKING POWDER BISCUIT
1900

1 qt. flour; butter size of an egg; 3 heaping teaspoonsful baking powder, and 1 of salt. Make a soft dough of sweet milk (or water), cut out, bake in a quick oven.

HOMINY FRITTERS

1 pint hot boiled hominy
½ tsp. salt
1 tbsp. flour
2 eggs
1 tbsp. baking powder
A little milk

Thin with a little cold milk; mix well and fry in deep hot fat to a light brown.

CORN MEAL MUSH — BUTTERED

1 qt. of water, pinch of salt, 1 cup corn meal, 2 tbsp. butter — place salt and water in top part of a double boiler, and bring to boiling point; add the corn meal gently and cook to mush; stirring constantly until smooth and thickened. After which it may be cooked over boiling water and cooked with occasional stirring for 25 minutes. Then beat in the butter. The mush may be served with cream and sugar.

CRACKLING CORN BREAD

1½ cups yellow cornmeal
½ tsp. of salt
½ cup of flour
2 tsp. sugar
1½ cups cracklins
2 eggs well beaten
3 tsp. of baking powder
¾ tsp. baking soda
1½ cups sour milk

Add flour, cornmeal, sugar, salt, baking powder, baking soda, and cracklins. Beat eggs and milk, mix well. Add to dry mixture. Bake in well greased iron skillet in hot oven until brown.

EGG CORN BREAD

Mrs. J. M. Peacock, 1891

Sift one quart meal, ⅓ tsp. soda, and one pinch salt, and mix with one pint sour milk, ½ tbsp. melted lard, and one egg, well beaten; mix thoroughly and bake in a quick oven.

NARCISSA COTHRAN'S SPOON BREAD

ca. 1850

¾ cup yellow cornmeal
1 tsp. salt
3 tbsp. melted butter
1 cup boiling water

1 cup milk
2 eggs well beaten with
   2 tsp. baking powder

Combine ingredients in order given and pour into 10-inch buttered casserole and bake for 40 minutes in moderate oven.

DOUGHNUTS

Work together four ounces of butter and six ounces of sugar; add by degrees three eggs; put in ½ pint of milk, a tsp. of baking powder and 1½ lbs. of flour. Roll out, cut and fry in grease; Grease should not be too hot, but just so that a bluish smoke rises from it.

LONE STAR DOUGHNUTS

4 cups all purpose flour
1 tsp. baking soda
1 tsp. salt
1 cup sour milk

2 eggs
¼ cup of lard or butter
1 cup sugar

Sift and measure flour, sift again with baking soda and salt. Beat eggs slightly, combine beaten eggs, shortening sugar and sour milk, mix well. Roll out and cut with floured donut cutter. Fry in deep fat—that will brown a cube of bread in 60 seconds. Drain and sprinkle with sugar.

ALL GRAHAM FLOUR BISCUITS

2 cups graham flour (whole wheat), 4 tsp. baking powder, 1 cup sweet milk, 1 egg, 1 tbsp. shortening, ½ tsp. salt. Drop from spoon onto a greased pan. Medium oven.

CORN MEAL GRIDDLE CAKES

1 pint corn meal (2 cups)
1 pint butter milk
1 tsp. soda
1 tsp. salt
2 eggs

Clabber milk may be used in place of butter milk. Mix and beat well.

GRIDDLE CAKES
(Very special, only made when flour was available.)

3 eggs
3 tbsp. butter
1 tsp. salt
3 cups sour milk
3 cups flour
2 level tsp. soda

Beat yolks of eggs, add salt, butter, milk and the flour into which the soda has been sifted and the egg white's just before baking. Beat and mix well.

WATERMELON SYRUP

Take the pulp of several sweet melons, crush and strain. Boil the juice slowly until of the desired consistency. Use syrup for hot cakes or biscuits.

HOW TO COOK RANCH GRIDDLE CAKES

Our bread was considered the staff of life and was made to perfection. I think that this must have been handed down from the first old wood cook stove, that my great-great-grandmother ever used. — Alline Halliburton Elliot

Griddle cakes were cooked on the eye of the old wood cook stove. Grease the eye of the stove with a piece of salt fat pork on the end of a fork. Have the stove hot before beginning to fry the cakes. Beat the griddle cakes thoroughly to ensure their perfection. Separate the eggs, whipping the yolks to a thick cream, and adding the whites beaten to a stiff froth just before baking.

Try a little of the batter first, to be sure it is all right, and the stove of the required heat. Allow one tbsp. of batter to each cake. If the cakes are doughy inside, the stove is too hot. If dry and tough, it is not hot enough. Griddle cakes are suppose to be light, thick and spongy. Never turn cakes the second time when cooking. Stack on hot plate when done.

PEARL DONEGAN'S GRIDDLE PANCAKES

1 cup cornmeal
½ cup all purpose flour
¼ tsp. salt
¼ tsp. baking soda
¼ tsp. baking powder
1 tsp. sugar
1 large egg
2 tbsp. lard
1 cup buttermilk
(milk to thin if needed)

Mix dry ingredients, add egg, oil, buttermilk, beat, and mix well. Heat griddle, test batter, thin with milk if needed. Test first cake and reduce heat as needed.

HOMEMADE BREAD STARTER
FOR PERPETUAL YEAST

1 pint flour
3 tbsp. sugar
Enough water to make a batter

Keep in a warm place for about three days or until it ferments and rises like bread sponge. It is then ready for use. Save a tbsp. of sponge for each loaf of bread to be baked and add 1 tbsp. sugar to each tbsp. of sponge (or to each loaf of bread). Keep in a jar in a cool place. If preferred, yeast cakes can be made by adding enough meal to a cup of sponge to enable it to be rolled and cut into cakes and dried.

HOE CAKE

Scald one quart of Indian-meal in enough water to make a thick batter; add a tsp. of salt, one of molasses, and two of butter. Bake on a board before a hot fire or in a pan.

PERPETUAL YEAST BREAD

First—to set the sponge pour "Starter" in a gallon porcelain or granite vessel. Add 3 cups lukewarm water, ⅓ cup sugar and enough flour to make a thick batter. Let rise until light and foamy, then it is ready for bread. Pour off 1 cupful for next starter.

To make the bread: Sift flour into tray or mixing bowl. Pour in sponge, add 1 tsp. salt, 2 tbsp. sugar, ½ cup lard or shortening. Work to medium stiff dough and put in greased vessel to rise. When twice its bulk, knead into loaves and put in a greased baking pan. When twice its bulk put in oven and bake 45 minutes.

CHEESE STRAWS

¾ lb. grated cheese
1 cup sifted flour
¼ cup butter

½ tsp. salt
1 tbsp. thick cream
Dash of cayenne pepper (¹⁄₁₆ tsp.)

Make a very stiff dough, roll one fourth of an inch thick and cut.

STOLLEN

Stollen is served in every German Texan's home throughout the Christmas season.

4¼ cups sifted flour
3 tsp. baking powder
1 tsp. salt
1 cup sugar
1 tsp. nutmeg
¼ tsp. cardamon
1 cup butter, (chilled)
    cut in small bits
8 oz. cottage cheese
2 eggs, beaten

1 tsp. vanilla
1 tsp. almond extract
¾ cups currants
1 cup golden raisins
½ cup dark rum
½ cup slivered almonds or
    chopped pecans
4 oz. slivered citron
2 tsp. grated lemon rind, fresh

In a very large mixing bowl, sift together all the dry ingredients. Add the bits of butter and cut into flour mixture. Drain the cottage cheese, put in a sieve if dry is not available—blend with the eggs and flavoring. Soak the currants and raisins in rum (do this ahead of time). Add the cheese, egg and flavoring mixture to the flour mixture and knead into a smooth dough. Work in the currants and raisins. Add more flour, if necessary. Blend in the almonds, citron and lemon rind. Knead well. Divide dough into 2 parts and shape each into a thick loaf. Place in greased loaf pans and brush with melted butter. Bake about 40 minutes in moderate oven (350 degrees). Remove from pans and cool on rack. Store in an airtight container. Spread the cut slices with butter.

SALT RISING BREAD

Start at 12 o'clock on short days, and at sun-down on long days.

1 cup sweet milk, let come to a boil. Pour corn meal enough to make a stiff sponge, a little thicker than batter cakes. Put in a warm place in small pitcher and cover tightly. Next morning take 3 teacups boiling water, pinch of salt, tbsp. soda level full, put flour in this enough to make a good batter, then pour sponge in this. Set batter in warm water, hot enough to bear your hand in it, and let stand until it rises. When it comes to top of pan or is light and foamy, mix ½ gal. of flour, more salt, 2 tbsp. shortening, and knead until it blisters, then put to rise again in a warm place. Let rise until nearly top of pan. Cook in steady oven about 40 minutes.

SCOTCH SHORT-CAKE

Two pounds of fine flour, one pound of fresh sweet butter, half a pound of finest sifted sugar; thoroughly knead together without water; roll out to half an inch in thickness, and place it on paper in a shallow pan; bake very slowly until of proper crispness. The cake, to be good, must be very brittle.

JOHNNY CAKES

One quart of buttermilk or sour milk, one quart Indian meal, one quart of flour, one cup of molasses, a tsp. of soda, two scant tsp. if the milk is sour, a tsp. of salt. Bake in shallow pans in a quick oven.

PUMPKIN BREAD

Stew and strain a sufficient quantity of pumpkin; add enough Indian-meal to stiffen it, with yeast and a little salt; when sufficiently raised, bake as in ordinary bread.

PINEAPPLE NUT BREAD

(Mrs. Wiley J. Peace, wife of Wiley J. Peace who organized the Williamson Co., TX, Bowies — 4th Regiment Rangers)

2 cups flour
½ cup sugar
½ tsp. salt
1 cup raisins
1 cup crushed pineapple

¾ cup chopped nuts
1 egg beaten
1 tsp. vanilla
2 tbsp. melted shortening
1 tsp. baking soda

Sift flour, sugar, baking powder, and salt into mixing bowl. Add raisins and nuts. Combine egg, vanilla and shortening and add to mixture. Dissolve soda in pineapple and add to mixture. Stir just until blended. Pour into greased loaf pan and bake in preheated moderate oven for 1 hour 20 minutes.

RICE BREAD

After a pint of rice has been boiled soft, mix it with two quarts of rice flour or wheat flour. When cold, add half a tsp. of yeast, a tsp. of salt, and enough milk to make a soft dough. When it has risen, bake in small buttered pans.

MILK TOAST

Toast the bread an even, delicate brown, and pile into a hot dish. Boil milk with a little salt, a tsp. of flour, and one of butter, rubbed together; pour it over the toast and serve hot.

CORN BREAD
1899

Two cups of sifted meal, half a cup of flour, two cups of sour milk, two well beaten eggs, half a cup of molasses or sugar, a tsp. of salt, two tbsp. of melted butter. Mix the meal and flour smoothly and gradually with the milk, then the butter, molasses and salt, then the beaten eggs, and lastly dissolve a level teaspoonful of baking soda in a little milk and beat thoroughly altogether. Bake nearly an hour in well buttered tins, not very shallow. This recipe can be made with sweet milk by using baking powder in place of soda.

SPIDER CORN CAKE

Beat two eggs and ¼ cup sugar together. Then add one cup sweet milk and one cup of sour milk in which you have dissolved one tsp. soda. Add a tsp. of salt. Then mix 1⅔ cups of granulated corn meal and ⅓ cup flour with this. Put a spider or skillet on the range and when it is hot, melt in two tbsp. of butter. Turn the spider so that the butter can run upon the sides of the pan. Pour in the corn cake mixture and add one more cup of sweet milk, but do not stir afterwards. Put this in the oven and bake from twenty to thirty-five minutes. When done, there should be a streak of custard through it.

CORN DODGERS

Mix with cold water into a soft dough one quart of southern corn meal, sifted, a tsp. of salt, a tbsp. of butter or lard melted. Mold into oval cakes with the hands and bake in a very hot oven, in well-greased pans. To be eaten hot. The crust should be brown.

RAISED POTATO-CAKE

Potato-cakes, to be served with roast lamb or with game, are made of equal quantities of mashed potatoes and of flour, say one quart of each, two tbsp. of butter, a little salt and milk enough to make a batter as for griddle-cakes; to this allow half a teacupful of fresh yeast; let it rise till it is light and bubbles of air form; then dissolve half a tsp. of soda in a spoonful of warm water and add to the batter; bake in muffin tins. These are good also with fricasseed chicken; take them from the tins and drop in the gravy just before sending to table.

EGG BISCUIT

Sift together a quart of dry flour and three heaping teaspoonfuls of baking powder. Rub into this thoroughly a piece of butter the size of an egg; add two well-beaten eggs, a tbsp. of sugar, a tsp. of salt. Mix all together quickly into a soft dough, with one cup of milk, or more if needed. Roll out nearly half of an inch thick. Cut into biscuits, and bake immediately in a quick oven from fifteen to twenty minutes.

SALLY LUNN

Rub a piece of butter as large as an egg into a quart of flour; add a tumbler of milk, two eggs, three tsp. of sugar, three tbsp. of baking powder and a tsp. of salt. Scatter the baking powder, salt and sugar into the flour; add the eggs, the butter melted, the milk. Stir all together and bake in well-greased round pans. Eat warm with butter.

SCOTCH SCONES

Thoroughly mix, while dry, one quart of sifted flour, loosely measured, with two heaping teaspoonfuls of baking powder; then rub into it a tbsp. of cold butter and a tsp. of salt. Be sure that the butter is well worked in. Add sweet milk enough to make a very soft paste. Roll out the paste about a quarter of an inch thick, using plenty of flour on the paste-board and rolling pin. Cut it into triangular pieces, each side about four inches long. Flour the sides and bottom of a biscuit tin, and place the pieces on it. Bake immediately in a quick oven from twenty to thirty minutes. When half done, brush over with sweet milk. Some cooks prefer to bake them on a floured griddle, and cut them a round shape the size of a saucer, then scarred across to form four quarters.

FLANNEL CAKES

Heat a pint of sweet milk and into it put two heaping tablespoonfuls of butter, let it melt, then add a pint of cold milk and the well beaten yolks of four eggs—placing the whites in a cool place; also a tsp. of salt, four tbsp. of home-made yeast and sufficient flour to make a stiff batter; set it in a warm place to rise; let it stand three hours or over night; before baking add the beaten whites; bake like any other griddle-cakes. Be sure to make the batter stiff enough, for flour must not be added after it has risen, unless it is allowed to rise again. These, half corn meal and half wheat, are very nice.

APPLE FRITTERS
ca. 1898

Make a batter in the proportion of one cup sweet milk to two cups flour, a heaping tsp. of baking powder, two eggs beaten separately, one tbsp. of sugar and a saltspoon of salt; heat the milk a little more than milk-warm, add it slowly to the beaten yolks and sugar; then add flour and whites of the eggs; stir all together and throw in thin slices of good sour apples, dipping the batter up over them; drop into boiling hot lard in large spoonfuls with pieces of apple in each, and fry to a light brown. Serve with maple syrup, or a nice syrup made with clarified sugar.

Bananas, peaches, sliced oranges and other fruits can be used in the same batter.

CRULLERS

This was a Christmas treat in the long ago.

Two cups sugar, three eggs, one cup sweet milk, butter the size of an egg, one half nutmeg, two tsp. yeast powders, enough flour to make like biscuit dough, roll dough real thin, cut in strips and fry in very hot lard.

To make real fancy, cut dough in very thin strips and braid then fry in hot lard.

CRACKLING BREAD

When making hog lard, trim the fat, leave no skin on, cook until a light brown, and the lard is cooked from the fat. The brown pieces that are left are called Cracklings. Using the regular recipe for Corn Pone, to the meal mixture, add one half as much cracklings as you have dough, fashion into pones and bake over a slow fire.

BREAD, CAMP FIRE STYLE

Old cowboys of generations ago gave us this method of making bread on the range.

Disregarding all frills and getting down to fundamentals, he advises dispensing with such articles as mixing bowls. Just lay your sack of flour flat side down on the ground. With a knife cut two gashes to form a cross in the side of the sack, after scooping out a hollow place in the flour, place therein a tsp. of salt, two tsp. of baking powder, a chunk of shortening as big as your fist, mix with a cupful of water and work in all the flour it will take to make a stiff dough. Pinch off goodly size hunks of the dough and twist around a green stick and hold over the camp fire until done. The hole in the sack of flour should be drawn together and tied tightly which will keep the remainder of the flour intact until next baking time.

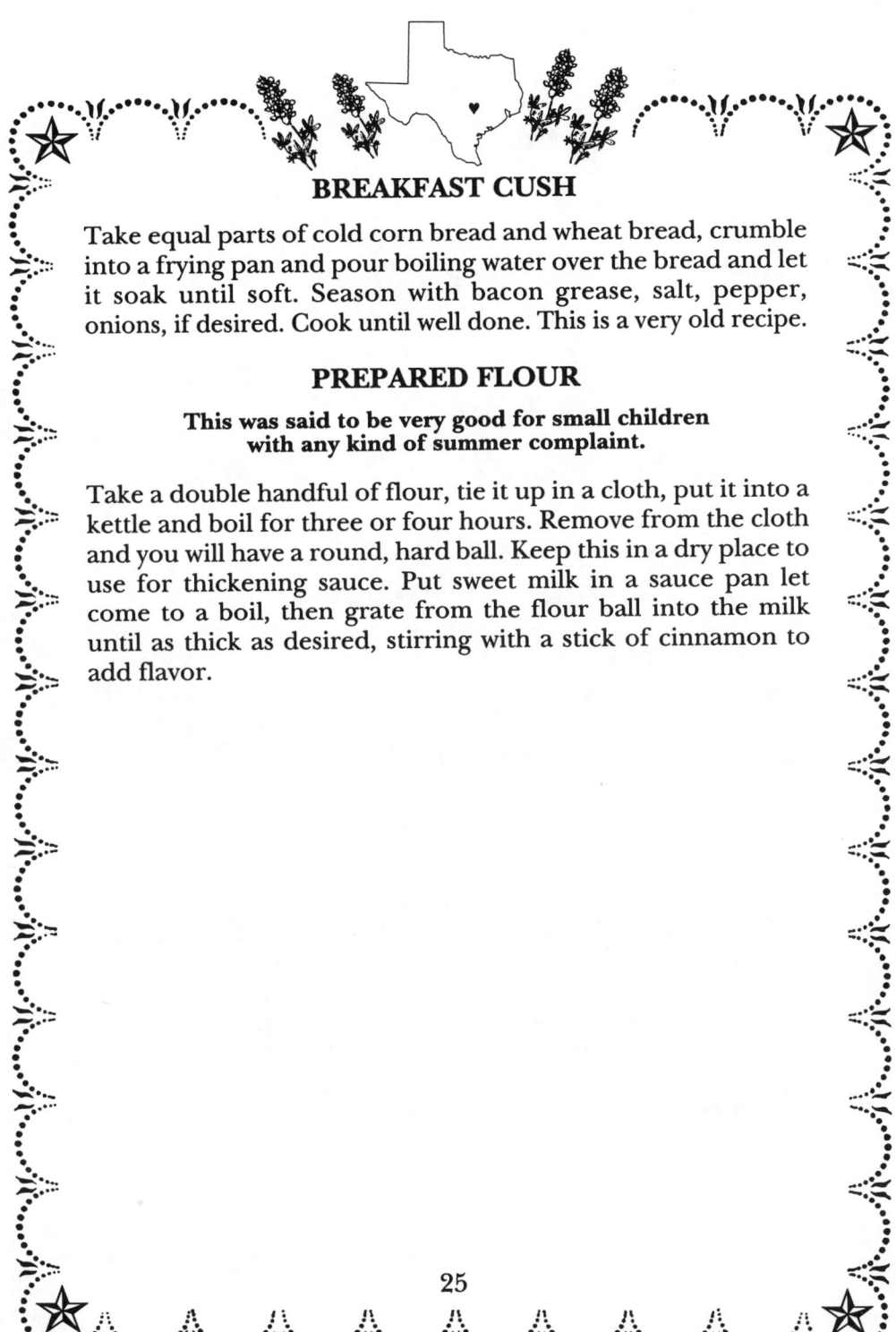

BREAKFAST CUSH

Take equal parts of cold corn bread and wheat bread, crumble into a frying pan and pour boiling water over the bread and let it soak until soft. Season with bacon grease, salt, pepper, onions, if desired. Cook until well done. This is a very old recipe.

PREPARED FLOUR

This was said to be very good for small children with any kind of summer complaint.

Take a double handful of flour, tie it up in a cloth, put it into a kettle and boil for three or four hours. Remove from the cloth and you will have a round, hard ball. Keep this in a dry place to use for thickening sauce. Put sweet milk in a sauce pan let come to a boil, then grate from the flour ball into the milk until as thick as desired, stirring with a stick of cinnamon to add flavor.

Soups

BEEF SOUP WITH OKRA

Cut a round steak in small pieces and fry in three tbsp. of butter, together with one sliced onion until very brown; put into a soup kettle with four qts. of cold water, and boil slowly an hour; add salt, pepper, and one pint of sliced okra and simmer three and one-half hours longer. Strain before serving

CORNED BEEF SOUP

ca. 1897

When the liquor in which corned beef and vegetables have been boiled is cold, remove all the grease that has risen and hardened on the top, and add tomatoes and tomato catsup and boil half an hour—thus making an excellent tomato soup; or add to it rice, or sago, or pearl barley, or turn it into a vegetable soup by boiling in the liquor any vegetables that are fancied. Several varieties of soups may have this stock for a basis and be agreeable to the taste.

MUTTON BROTH

After the steaks have been cut from the leg, the lower part is just adapted for a soup. The neckpiece is also very nice. Boil the meat very gently in cold water, adding a turnip, a carrot, and a spoonful of rice. All the fat should be removed. Toward the last, add a little minced parsley. Dumplings are an excellent addition.

BLACK BEAN SOUP

Three lbs. soup bone, one qt. black beans, soaked over night and drained; one onion chopped fine; juice of one lemon. Pepper, salt, and Durkee's Challenge Sauce to taste. Boil the soup bone, beans, and onions together six hours; strain, and add seasoning. Slice lemon and put on top when served.

TOMATO SOUP

Take a knuckle of veal, a bony piece of beef, a neck of mutton, or almost any piece of meat you may happen to have; set it over the fire in a small quantity of water, cover it closely, and boil very gently, to extract the juices of the meat. When nearly done, add a quantity of peeled tomatoes and stew till the tomatoes are done; add salt and pepper to your taste. This is a very cheap, healthful, and easily made soup.

FARM OX-TAIL SOUP

Parboil in some water two ox-tails and cut the meat in small pieces, melt two oz. of butter, fry in two small onions, one turnip, two carrots, half a stalk of celery, two slices of bacon; cut up fine. Add to the liquor in which the ox-tails have been parboiled, one tsp. of extract of beef, then add the fried vegetables and thicken with two oz. of flour, adding a tbsp. of Worchestshire sauce; Boil up, strain, add the cut ox-tail, and serve with grated rusk.

BEEF TEA

**Grandmothers Ruth Minerva Wisdom Miller
and Mrs. Peter Hagan**

1 stick butter	3 carrots sliced
4 lbs. beef scraps or soup meat (boil)	2 stalks celery
	1 bell pepper quartered
8 lbs. beef and veal bones	2 bay leaves
3 peeled onions, sliced	3 sprigs parsley
1 turnip	1 tsp. whole black pepper
2 tbsp. salt	3 qts. of water

Melt the butter in a large soup pot and brown the meat plus bones with the onions. Add all remaining ingredients. Simmer four hours, skinning the fat off the top from time to time. Strain—makes 2 quarts.

SQUIRREL SOUP

Wash and quarter three or four good sized squirrels; put them on, with a small tbsp. of salt, directly after breakfast, in a gallon of cold water. Cover the pot close, and set it on the back part of the stove to simmer gently, not boil. Add vegetables just the same as you do in case of other meat soups in the summer season, but especially good will you find corn, Irish potatoes, tomatoes and Lima beans. Strain the soup through a coarse colander when the meat has boiled to shreds, so as to get rid of the squirrels' troublesome little bones. Then return to the pot, and after boiling a while longer, thicken with a piece of butter rubbed in flour. Celery and parsley leaves chopped up are also considered an improvement by many. Toast two slices of bread, cut them into dice one-half inch square, fry them in butter, put them into the bottom of your tureen, and then pour the soup boiling hot upon them. Very good.

GUMBO OR OKRA SOUP

Fry out the fat of a slice of bacon or fat ham, drain it off, and in it fry the slices of a large onion, brown; scald, peel and cut up two qts. fresh tomatoes, when in season. Cut thin one qt. okra; put them, together with a little chopped parsley, in a stew-kettle with about three qts. of hot broth of any kind; cook slowly for three hours, season with salt and pepper. Serve hot.

In chicken broth the same quantity of okra pods, used for thickening instead of tomatoes, forms a chicken gumbo soup.

FORCE MEAT BALL SOUP

One cupful of cooked veal or fowl meat, minced; mix with this a handful of fine bread crumbs, the yolks of four hard-boiled eggs rub smooth together with a tbsp. of milk; season with pepper and salt; add a half tsp. of flour, and bind all together with two beaten eggs; the hands to be well floured, and the mixture to be made into little balls the size of a nutmeg; drop into the soup about twenty minutes before serving.

FISH SOUP
1897

Select large, fine fish, clean it thoroughly, put it over the fire with a sufficient quantity of water, allowing for each pound of fish one qt. of water; add an onion cut fine and a bunch of sweet herbs. When the fish is cooked, and is quite tasteless, strain all through a colander, return to the fire, add some butter, salt and pepper to taste. A small tbsp. of Worcestershire sauce may be added if liked. Serve with small squares of fried bread and thin slices of lemon.

BOUILLON

A twenty-cent soup bone simmered in a large kettle of water, six or eight hours. Remove the meat, strain the liquor and set away until morning. Remove the fat which has risen. Put the stock on to boil. Just before taking up, add a tbsp. of caramel to give it an amber color. Season with salt and pepper.

CARAMEL FOR SOUP

Put a teacup of sugar in a small frying pan and set over the fire. Stir occasionally until it is a bright brown color and sends forth a burning smell. Add a half pint of vinegar, boil and when cool, bottle. Add to soups at discretion

Butter, Cheese, and Eggs

TO MAKE BUTTER QUICKLY

Immediately after the cow is milked, strain the milk into clean pans, and set it over a moderate fire until it is scalding hot; do not let it boil; then set it aside; when it is cold, skim off the cream; the milk will still be fit for any ordinary use.

When you have enough cream put it into a clean earthen basin; beat it with a wooden spoon until the butter is made, which will not be long; then take it from the milk and work it with a little cold water until it is free from milk; then drain off the water, put a small tbsp. of fine salt to each lb. of butter and work it in. A small tsp. of fine white sugar, worked in with the salt, will be found an improvement—sugar is a great preservative. Make the butter in a roll; cover it with a bit of muslin and keep it in a cold place. A reliable recipe.

COTTAGE CHEESE

Put a pan of sour or loppered milk on the stove or range where it is not too hot; let it scald until the whey rises to the top (be careful that it does not boil, or the curd will become hard and tough). Place a clean cloth or towel over a sieve and pour this whey and curd into it, leaving it covered to drain two or three hours; then put it into a dish and chop it fine with a spoon, adding a tsp. of salt, a tbsp. of butter and enough sweet cream to make the cheese the consistency of putty. With your hands make it into little balls flattened. Keep it in a cool place. Many like it made rather thin with cream, serving it in a deep dish.

CHEESE SOUFFLE

Melt an ounce of butter in a saucepan; mix smoothly with it one ounce of flour, a pinch of salt and cayenne and a quarter of a pint of milk; simmer the mixture gently over the fire, stirring it all the time, till it is as thick as melted butter, stir into it about three ounces of finely grated cheese. Turn it into a basin and mix with it the yolks of two well beaten eggs. Whisk three whites to a solid froth, and just before the souffle is baked put them into it, and pour the mixture into a small round tin. It should be only half filled as the fondu will rise very high. Pin a napkin around the dish in which it is baked, and serve the moment it is baked. It would be well to have a metal cover strongly heated. Time twenty minutes. Sufficient for six persons.

SCALLOPED CHEESE

Take three slices of bread well-buttered, first cutting off the brown outside crust. Grate fine a quarter of a pound of any kind of good cheese; lay the bread in layers in a buttered baking dish, sprinkle over it the grated cheese, some salt and pepper to taste. Mix four well beaten eggs with three cups of milk; pour it over the bread and cheese. Bake it in a hot oven as you would cook a bread pudding. This makes an ample dish for four people.

CAYENNE CHEESE STRAWS

A quarter of a pound of flour, two ounces butter, two ounces grated cheese, a pinch of salt and a few grains of cayenne pepper. Mix into a paste with the yolk of an egg. Roll out to the thickness of a silver quarter, about four or five inches long; cut into strips about a third of an inch wide, twist them as you would a paper spill and lay them on a baking sheet slightly floured. Bake in a moderate oven until crisp, but they must not be the least brown. If put away in a tin, these cheese straws will keep a long time. Serve cold, piled tastefully on a glass dish.

WELSH RAREBIT

Grate three ounces of dry cheese and mix it with the yolks of two eggs, put four ounces of grated bread and three of butter; beat the whole together in a mortar with a dessert spoonful of made mustard, a little salt and some pepper; toast some slices of bread, cut off the outside crust, cut it in shapes and spread the paste thick upon them. Put them in the oven, let them become hot and slightly browned, serve as hot as possible.

SHIRRED EGGS

Set into the oven until quite hot a common white dish large enough to hold the number of eggs to be cooked, allowing plenty of room for each. Melt in it a small piece of butter, and breaking the eggs carefully in a saucer, one at a time, slip them into the hot dish; sprinkle over them a small quantity of pepper and salt and allow them to cook four or five minutes. Adding a tbsp. of cream for every two eggs, when the eggs are first slipped in, is a great improvement.

This is far more delicate than fried eggs. Or prepare the eggs the same and set them in a steamer over boiling water.

APPLE OMELET

Apple Omelet, to be served with broiled sparerib or roast pork, is very delicate. Take nine large, tart apples, four eggs, one cup of sugar, one tbsp. of butter; add cinnamon or other spices to suit your taste; stew the apples till they are very soft; mash them so that there will be no lumps; add the butter and sugar while they are still warm; but let them cool before putting in the beaten eggs; bake this till it is brown; you may put it all in a shallow pudding-dish or in two tin plates to bake. Very good.

CHEESE FONDUE
Mrs. A. E. Haricht, 1891

One cup bread crumbs, very dry and fine; two scant cups of milk, fresh, or it will curdle; one-half pound dry old cheese grated; three eggs, whipped very light; one small tbsp. melted butter; pepper and salt; a pinch of soda dissolved in hot water and stirred into the milk. Soak the crumbs in the milk, beat into these the eggs, the butter, the seasoning, lastly the cheese. Butter a neat baking dish, pour the fondue into it, strew dry bread crumbs on the top, and bake in rather a quick oven until delicately browned. Serve immediately in the baking dish, as it soon falls.

BAKED OMELET

Beat the whites and yolks of four or six eggs separately; add to the yolks a small cup of milk, a tbsp. of flour or cornstarch, a tsp. of baking powder, ½ tsp. of salt, and, lastly, the stiff beaten whites. Bake in a well buttered pie tin or plate about half an hour in a steady oven. It should be served the moment it is taken from the oven, as it is liable to fall.

THE BEST EGG CUSTARD

Beat well 5 eggs; heat to boiling point 2½ cups milk, add slowly to eggs — continue beating and gradually add 1 cup sugar, 1 tbsp. of vanilla extract, pinch of salt. Pour into baking dish, sit in pan of water, and place in oven (medium hot). Cook until broom straw comes out clean. Or bake in unbaked pie crust. This custard is very good for a diet in the sick room.

MUSHROOM OMELET
ca. 1900

6 eggs
¼ cup mushrooms
1½ tbsp. of butter

Stew the mushrooms a few minutes. Then chop them fine. Make a plain omelet. When it is ready to fold, place the mushrooms across the center, fold twice over, let it cook two minutes longer, and serve hot.

HAM OMELET
ca. 1900

4 eggs
½ tsp. flour
2 tbsp. milk
2 tbsp. chopped ham
½ grated onion
1 tbsp. chopped parsley
Salt and pepper to taste

Beat the yolks to a cream, and add the other ingredients. Rub all these smoothly together, and then add the whites of eggs, beaten to a froth. Beat all thoroughly together. Put a tbsp. of butter in the frying pan. When it melts add the omelet. Let it stand, shaking occasionally to prevent from sticking to the pan, till the eggs are quite set. Then fold as in a plain omelet (roll the omelet, folding it in two or three rolls and making it long and narrow.) It is always easier to make several small omelets and have them pretty and sightly, than to succeed perfectly in making a large one, turn into a hot dish and serve.

Fish

HURRICANE OYSTERS

Used by Nancy Kincheloe Green, James and Gustavus E. Green, 1854

History doesn't include a reference to any breading, but we suggest corn or cracker meal. Mr. Green remembered this as the best breakfast he ever had!

The Green family of Matagorda County survived a major storm hitting this area in 1854. They weathered the storm by "planting" the children in the sand. Gus Green a lad of nine, later related to his grandchildren, his discovering a pot and slab of bacon in the debris. The children gathered oysters from the beach while their cook rendered drippings from the bacon which was used to fry the oysters.

BROILED SHAD

Scrape, split, wash, and dry the shad on a cloth; season with pepper and salt; grease the gridiron well; as soon as it is hot lay the shad on to broil with the inside downward. One side being well browned, turn it. It should broil a quarter of an hour or more according to thickness. Butter well and send to table hot.

BAKED SHAD

Many people are of the opinion that the very best method of cooking a shad is to bake it. Stuff it with bread-crumbs, salt, pepper, butter, and parsley, and mix this up with beaten yolk of egg; fill the fish with it and sew it up or fasten a string around it. Pour over it a little water and some butter, and bake as you would a fowl. A shad will require from an hour to an hour and a quarter to bake.

BROILED SALMON

The steaks from the center of the fish are best. Sprinkle with salt and pepper, spread on a little butter, and broil over a clear but slow fire.

BAKED SALMON WITH CREAM SAUCE
1898

Butter a sheet of foolscap paper on both sides, and wrap the fish up in it, pinning the ends securely together. Lay in the baking-pan, and pour six or seven spoonfuls of butter-and-water over it. Turn another pan over all, and steam in a moderate oven.

SALMON CROQUETTES
Mrs. John Webb, 1891

One can of salmon. Turn into a vessel (not tin) for awhile before using, to "air." Use two-thirds as much rolled cracker crumbs as you have salmon. Butter the size of the yolk of an egg melted in one-half cup of water. Pepper, salt and a few drops of lemon juice. Sift the rolled crackers, using coarser part to the salmon, finer to roll the croquettes in. After mixing ingredients thoroughly, mold, roll in beaten egg, then cracker crumbs. Fry in hot lard.

FISH BALLS

Two cupfuls cold boiled codfish, fresh or salted. Chop the fish when you have freed it of bones and skin; work in one cupful of mashed potatoes, and moisten with a half cup of drawn butter with an egg beaten in. Season to taste. Have them soft enough to mold, yet firm enough to keep in shape. Roll the balls in flour, and fry quickly to a golden-brown in lard or clean dripping. Take from the fat so soon as they are done; lay in a colander or sieve and shake gently, to free them from every drop of grease. Turn out for moment on white paper to absorb any lingering drops, and serve on a hot dish.

HALIBUT CUTLETS

Cut your halibut steaks an inch thick, wipe them with a dry cloth, and season with salt and cayenne pepper. Have ready a pan of yelk of eggs (3 yolks of eggs) well beaten and a dish of grated bread-crumbs. Put some fresh lard or beef drippings in a frying-pan and hold it over the fire till it boils. Dip your cutlets in the egg, and then in the bread-crumbs. Fry a light brown; serve up hot. Salmon or any large fish may be fried in the same manner.

FISH FRITTERS

Take a piece of salt codfish, pick it up very fine, put it into a saucepan, with plenty of cold water; bring it to a boil, turn off the water, and add another of cold water; bring it to a boil; let this boil with the fish about fifteen minutes, very slowly; strain off this water, making the fish quite dry, and set aside to cool. In the meantime, stir up a batter of a pint of milk, four eggs, a pinch of salt, one large teaspoonful of baking powder in flour, enough to make thicker than batter cakes. Stir in the fish and fry like any fritters. Very fine accompaniment to a good breakfast.

STEWED TERRAPIN, WITH CREAM
1897

Place in a saucepan, two heaping tbsp. of butter and one of dry flour; stir it over the fire until it bubbles; then gradually stir in a pint of cream, a tsp. of salt, a quarter of a tsp. of white pepper, the same of grated nutmeg, and a very small pinch of cayenne. Next, put in a pint of terrapin meat and stir all until it is scalding hot. Move to the saucepan to the back part of the stove or range, where the contents will keep hot but not boil; then stir in four well-beaten yolks of eggs; do not allow the terrapin to boil after adding the eggs, but pour it immediately into a tureen containing a gill of good Madeira and a tbsp. of lemon juice. Serve hot.

ENTREE OF SHRIMPS AND TOMATOES
Mrs. Tallichet, 1891

Fry four slices of breakfast slip brown and to the fat add one can of tomatoes; stew three-quarters of an hour. Have one can of Baratara shrimps washed in cold water, well drained and any shells carefully removed; sprinkle them with one-third of a tbsp. of cayenne, a pinch of black pepper, and a little salt. Put in a baking dish, add the tomatoes, cover with a layer of stale bread crumbs, grated. Drop small bits of butter on top then put in oven and brown nicely.

TO MAKE A CRAB PIE

Procure the crabs alive, put them in boiling water, along with some salt. Boil them for a quarter of an hour or twenty minutes, according to the size. When cold, pick the meat from the claws and body. Chop all together, and mix it with crumbs of bread, pepper and salt, and a little butter. Put all this into the shell and brown in a hot oven. A crab shell will hold the meat of two crabs.

ROAST CLAMS IN THE SHELL
1897

Roast in a pan over a hot fire, or in a hot oven, or, at a "Clam Bake," on hot stones; when they open, empty the juice into a saucepan; add the clams, with butter, pepper and a very little salt.

FROGS FRIED
1897

Frogs are usually fried and are considered a great delicacy. Only the hind-legs and quarters are used. Clean them well, season, and fry in egg batter, or dip in beaten egg and fine cracker crumbs, the same as oysters.

Meat, Poultry, and Game

PIONEER MEALS ON THE TRAIL TO TEXAS

The pioneers came to Texas from the United States in oxcarts, horse and mule drawn wagons. Cooking was done over a camp fire. The menu for the three meals of the day varied little. Enough corn pone was usually cooked in the morning to last all day, also meat, such as venison, wild turkey, antelope, birds and other plentiful game. A bountiful supply of good honey from wild bee trees was very acceptable, as well as wild onions, lettuce, other greens, water cress and gherkins, which could be found in the woods and along the streams.

PIONEER STYLE MEAT

This recipe is a historic recipe; it is not recommended by the DRT for consumption.

Jerked meat was preserved meat of buffalo, bear, wild turkeys, and other wild game. The meat was cut in strips about an inch thick, then it was salted and peppered. After the sun was up in the morning, the meat was hung on the line to dry. It was brought into the house at night to keep the dew from falling on it.

If a rain came it was brought in. It required four or five days to cure the meat, depending upon the heat of the sun.

After it was cured, it was stored in clean sacks. (If the pesky flies were just too bad, someone was detailed with a tree branch to mind the flies away) until the meat became hard and dry.

In preparing jerked meat for cooking, it was soaked in water several hours, then cooked as fresh meat.

CORNBREAD DRESSING

1 cup chopped celery
½ cup chopped onion
¼ cup butter
1 tsp. poultry seasoning
½ tsp. sage

4 cups dry, cubed bread
4 cups crumbled cornbread
1 egg beaten
2½ cups chicken broth
Salt and pepper

Preheat oven to moderate temperature, grease 7" x 12" pan. Sauté celery and onion in butter; stir in seasonings, mix bread cubes and cornbread; add sautéed vegetables and egg; add broth, mix well. Bake 45 to 60 minutes. This will stuff a 10 to 12 lb. turkey — 16 servings.

☆ ☆ ☆

ADVICE FOR BOILING MEAT

When meat is to be boiled for eating, put it into boiling water at the beginning, by which its juices are preserved.

☆ ☆ ☆

SOUTHERN BOILED HAM

Put a handful of new hay into an iron pot of cold water. When the water comes to a boil, place the ham on top of the hay, then place a layer of hay on top of the ham. boil until tender, remove from the pot. Peel off the skin and pare off all discolorations, dust the ham liberally with flour or bread crumbs, a little ground cinnamon, sugar, pepper, and place in the oven and bake until brown. The new hay gives the ham a delicious flavor.

GRANDMA'S SUGAR CURE
1840

A historic recipe that is not recommended for consumption according to today's health standards – check with a nutritionist before eating.

12 pints salt
4 oz. salt petre
4 oz. red pepper

2 pints sugar
4 oz. black pepper
½ cup hot water

Mix all together well and rub hams shoulders and bacon thoroughly. Lay up on shelf for 3–4 days, turning every day. Hang and let dry. Wash in warm water before trimming and cutting to cook.

HAM STUFFED PEPPERS
Margaret Youngblood Stiles

½ cup cooked ham, chopped fine

½ cup bread crumbs

Mix with a pinch of salt, a bit of paprika, and a lump of butter the size of a walnut. Soften with sweet milk or stock. Remove seeds from peppers and fill. Bake covered with buttered crumbs until tender.

MEAT CURE
1840

A historic recipe that is not recommended for consumption according to today's health standards – check with nutritionist before eating.

To cure 250 lbs. of pork:
12½ lbs. of salt
1 lb. black pepper
½ lb. salt petre

2½ lbs. brown sugar
½ lb. red peppers

Mix ingredients together thoroughly. Lay meat in wooden box, taking care that pieces do not touch. Cover with mixture.

Let remain in mixture until dry. Use as needed. Wash in warm water before cutting. *Note:* While the ingredients are similar in these recipes, the methods of finishing the cure are different and the tastes of the meat are, too. Sometimes instead of making jerky of venison, the venison hams were cured with the sugar cure method.

SON-OF-A-GUN-STEW

Cut into cubes the liver, heart, and sweet breads of a buffalo, beef, venison or hog. Roll in meal and fry slightly. Cover with boiling water, add onion, salt and pepper, thicken with flour and cook slowly until meat falls to pieces and the liquor had stewed down low. Some cooks added some lean meat to these other ingredients.

SUMMER SAUSAGE

2 lb. ground beef	1 tsp. garlic salt
2 tbsp. curing salt	1 tsp. mustard seeds
1 tsp. pepper	1 cup water

Blend all ingredients. Make three rolls. Wrap in damp cloth and keep cold for 24 hours. Bake covered in a moderate oven for one hour. Let cool and serve.

DEEP FRIED CHICKEN

This recipe was prepared many times by my Maternal Grandmother Izella (Richardson) Lockhart. Granny cooked her fish and fried pies this way also. All year round – the time of year made no difference. She made these goodies for church socials, reunions, family get togethers, etc.; Granny made her chicken, fish and fried pies for all to enjoy and enjoy they did!

Cut up fryers and lard or suet	1 large iron cauldron
Equal amounts of corn meal and flour for batter	Wood for cooking

CHRISTMAS ROAST GOOSE

The goose should not be more than eight months old, and the fatter the more tender and juicy the meat. Stuff with the following mixture: Three pints of bread crumbs, six oz. of butter, or part butter and part salt pork, one tsp. each of sage, black pepper and salt, one chopped onion. Do not stuff very full, and stitch openings firmly together to keep flavor in and fat out. Place in a baking pan with a little water, and baste frequently with salt and water (some add vinegar); turn often so that the sides and back may be nicely browned. Bake two hours or more; when done take from the pan, pour off the fat, and to the brown gravy left add the chopped giblets which have previously been stewed until tender, together with the water they were boiled in; thicken with a little flour and butter rubbed together, bring to a boil and serve.

CHRISTMAS SEASON
WITH THE 2ND CAVALRY IN TEXAS
1855

Elizabeth (Eliza) Griffin Johnston with three of their children, Margaret (Maggie), Sid (Sidney) and McClung, accompanied her husband General Albert Sidney Johnston, Commander of the United States of America 2nd Cavalry Regiment from Jefferson Barracks, Mo., through Texas for duty on the Texas frontier. Robert E. Lee was second in command. They began the journey, October 27, 1855, and crossed the Red River into Texas at Preston, December 15, 1855. Elizabeth (Eliza) kept a diary while on the trip. The following excerpts are from this diary.

Monday, (Dec.) 17th   Marched 20 miles crossed the Mineral, a small stream, bought 20 pds of butter & 3 bush of Sweet Potatoes, & chickens also.

Tues. 18th   Marched 14 miles passed through Gainesville saw evidence of a tremendous hurricane which passed through and south

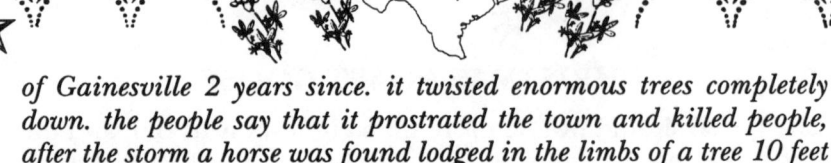

of Gainesville 2 years since. it twisted enormous trees completely down. the people say that it prostrated the town and killed people, after the storm a horse was found lodged in the limbs of a tree 10 feet from the ground . . .

Wednesday, 19th   Marched 18 miles had to burn a place to camp on, and the fire very nearly got the better of us, but the Pioneers conquered it.

Thursday, 20th   Marched 20 miles, clear weather a very badly watered country hardly enough for drinking, cooking, or half the horses.

Friday, 21st   Marched 14 miles had plenty of nice rain water standing in holes camped near Victoria peak, went on the top in the evening had a fine & extensive view discovered 2 or 3 miles distant a man who was lost 2 days since and for whom 3 men were sent to search he got safely into camp this evening.

Saturday 22nd   Marched 15 miles camped at Buffalo Springs Ellen (Irish maid) quite sick with dysentary, thought she was going to die last night & made me promise to keep Martin her nephew. at 8 o'clock the coldest norther I ever felt after a delightful spring day, all the fires had to be put out in camp and we found it impossible to keep warm. The thermometer 4 degrees below zero.

Sunday 23   Could not march the wind blowing almost a Hurricane and cold bitter cold had to take Ran and Ellen into our tent on account of the cold. they were nearly frozen. George (English driver) and little Martin crawled into the carriage, so cold we laid in bed till 12 o'clock in the day, and fed the children with cold bread and a slice of ____. Got up at 1 o'clock but did nothing but try to keep warm and could not succeed. Poor little Maggie crying with the cold and impossible to get near the fire the smoke whirling round in eddys nearly puts out our eyes. I sit with Maggie on my knee trying to keep her warm and roll Sid and Clung up in blankets went to bed at 6 o'clock without dinner or supper after giving little ones a few crackers. had a nice piece of antelope sent us by Mr Low yesterday. today it was frozen so hard we could not cut it with an axe. the water frozen and the men cut it out in blocks 6 inches thick, of clear solid ice. setting in a bucket by the fire it freezes so rapidly we can scarcely use it fast enough.

Monday 24th Marched 20 miles. camped and employed ourselves in keeping warm. gude man had a hole dug in the tent and filled with bright coals which kept us warm. Maggie sat down by it and said well Pa why did you not think of this before an express came into Camp Saturday night and brought 2 letters from Henny to the Genl.

Tuesday 25th Christmas I wonder if friends far away, with all their comforts now, can imagine us sleeping on the ground and shivering round a camp fire to keep life in us. So cold we could not march today. The officers have managed to have egg nog and have given the soldiers a dram apiece of whiskey We are now 35 miles from Belknap. The Genl received orders by the express to leave 4 companies at that place, and proceed at once to the Llano with the remaining 6 we are all distressed at the prospect of separation. and fear the Reg will not be together again. the officers all drank apple toddy with Lieut Johnson. we had for our dinner antelope venison roast Beef & Ham for our Xmas dinner. I opened Aunt Marys box for the first time as a Xmas gift for us and enjoyed the contents vastly. after Tattoo the Buglers came and serenaded us one of the buglers sings the Swiss Yodling sweetly I sent them some warm rolls and ham. & the officers sent them some whiskey our sentinel drew out a a [sic] miserable looking pone of bread, and said to Ran that they hurried him off so that he could not eat his supper so he snatched it up and ran off. I could not see him eat that for his Xmas fare so I made Ran give him some ham and bread.

Wednesday 26th My birthday. Marched 20 miles very cold. camped without water except a small demijon brought along for the children Dr Vollurn came from Belknap to meet us, says that in quarters the thermometer stood 2 degrees below zero, so it must have been infinitely colder where we were as we were 500 feet higher & exposed to the full blast of the gale. The poor sentinels suffered." [original spelling and punctuation]

Eliza Griffin Johnston painted the numerous Texas wildflowers along the Regiment's route in the warmer months. The original watercolor paintings are still as vivid and fresh as the day they were painted. She presented the watercolors or Texas flowers to her husband for his birthday in a leather bound volume. The children of General Johnston gave the book of paintings to the William Barret Travis Chapter of the Daughters of the Republic Museum after General Johnston's death. It is the most beautiful and prized of the museum collections. The DRT published a book of reproductions of her wildflower paintings; the colors are true to Eliza Griffin's wildflower paintings. DRT is now in the process of republishing, *Texas Wildflowers,* by Eliza Griffin Johnston (published first in 1972 and 1976). Eliza Griffin Johnston became a member of the Daughters of the Republic of Texas.

General Albert Sidney Johnston, a West Point graduate in June of 1826, came to Texas in 1836 and enlisted in the Texas Army as a private. In 1836, Johnston was appointed adjutant general by Thomas Jefferson Rusk. He became senior brigadier general in command of the Texas Army in 1837. Johnston was wounded in a duel with Felix Huston whom he was replacing and could not assume command of the Texas Army. He was appointed secretary of war of the Republic of Texas by President Mirabeau B. Lamar, December 22, 1838.

General Johnston was killed at the Battle of Shiloh, April 6, 1862.

HOW TO COOK YOUNG CHICKENS
Mrs. C. A. Trimble, 1891

Dress and joint them as usual. Place in a dripping pan and just cover with sweet cream, season with a little salt, pepper and a little butter; now set in the oven to cook and by the time the cream is almost cooked away the chicken will be done. They are splendid done this way.

FRIED CHICKEN WITH CREAM SAUCE
ca. 1901

1 Spring Chicken	1 tbsp. flour
3 tbsp. lard	½ pint milk

Clean and cut the chicken at the joints. Dredge well with salt and pepper, and a little flour. Put the lard into the frying pan, and when hot, add the chicken, letting it fry slowly for three-quarters of an hour until done. Be careful not to burn. When done, arrange the pieces on a hot dish. Pour off all the fat that remains in the frying pan but one tablespoonful. Add to this a tablespoonful of sifted flour. Mix thoroughly and then pour in a half pint of rich cream or milk. Season well with salt and pepper, let it come to a slight boil and pour over the chicken and serve.

CHICKEN CROQUETTES
Alice P. Tiller Littlefield, 1891

Boil two chickens until very tender, mince fine, and season with pepper, salt and one-half pint of cream or soup stock, yolks of two eggs, a cup and a half of boiled rice mixed with the meat and rolled in pieces one inch thick and three long. Then roll the croquettes in cracker crumbs and fry in hot lard to a nice brown, and serve in flat dish with boiled rice cooked so every grain seems whole. This is a convenient dish when the chicken is wanted in the bouillon.

PICKLED CHICKEN
1899

Boil four chickens till tender enough for meat to fall from bones; put meat in a stone jar and pour over it three pints of cold, good cider vinegar and a pint and a half of the water in which the chickens were boiled; add spices if preferred, and it will be ready for use in two days. This is a popular Sunday evening dish; it is good for luncheon at any time.

CHICKEN CHEESE
Mrs. James Ford, 1891

Take a chicken and cook very tender. Cook the gravy of the chicken down to a jell. Take out all the bones and chop fine. Season with salt and pepper, boil hard six eggs, chop the whites and yellows separately, then put a layer of chicken, then one of whites, then one of chicken and one of yellows, until the bowl is full, then pour the water it was cooked in over it; flavor with celery if desired.

CHICKEN PATTIES

Mince up fine cold chicken, either roasted or boiled. Season it with pepper and salt, and a little minced parsley and onion. Moisten it with chicken gravy or cream sauce, fill scalloped shells that are lined with pastry with the mixture, and sprinkle bread crumbs over the tops. Put two or three tiny pieces of butter over each, and bake brown in a hot oven.

BROILED CHICKEN ON TOAST
1899

Broil the usual way and when thoroughly done take it up in a square tin or dripping-pan, butter it well, season with pepper and salt and set it in the oven for a few minutes. Lay slices of moistened buttered toast on a platter; take the chicken up over it, add to the gravy in the pan part of a cupful of cream, if you have it; if not, use milk. Thicken with a little flour and pour over the chicken. This is considered most excellent.

BRAISED DUCK

Prepare a pair of fine young ducks, the same as for roasting, place them in a stewpan together with two or three slices of bacon, a carrot, an onion stuck with two cloves, and a little thyme and parsley. Season with pepper, and cover the whole with a broth, adding to the broth a gill of white wine. Place the pan over a gentle fire and allow the ducks to simmer until done, basting them frequently. When done remove them from the pan, and place them where they will keep hot. A turnip should then be cut up and fried in some butter. When nicely browned, drain the pieces and cook them until tender in the liquor in which the ducks were braised. Now strain and thicken the gravy, and after dishing up the ducks, pour it over them garnishing with the pieces of turnip.

DUCK PIE

Cut all the meat from cold roast ducks; cut the bones and stuffing into cold water; cover them and let boil; put the meat into a deep dish; pour on enough of the stock made from the bones to moisten; cover with pastry slit in the centre with a knife, and bake a light brown.

STEWED PIGEONS
1899

Clean and stuff with onion dressing, thyme, etc., — do not sew up; take five or more slices of corned pork, let it fry awhile in a pot so that the fat comes out and it begins to brown a little; then lay the pigeons all around in the fat, leaving the pork still in; add hot water enough to partially cover them; cover tightly and boil an hour or so until tender; then turn off some of the liquid and keep turning them so they will brown nicely; then heat and add the liquor poured off; add extra thyme, pepper, and keep turning until the pigeons and gravy are nicely browned. Thicken with a little flour, and serve with the gravy poured over them; garnish with parsley.

ROAST PARTRIDGES
Mrs. I. V. Davis, 1891

Pluck, singe, draw and truss three partridges. Roast for about twenty minutes, baste with butter; when the grease begins to run from them you may safely assume the partridges are done. Place then in a dish together with bread crumbs fried nicely and arranged in small heaps. Gravy should be served in a tureen apart.

PIGEON PIE

Take half a dozen pigeons; stuff each one with a dressing the same as for turkey; loosen the joints with a knife, but do not separate them. Put them in a stewpan with water enough to cover them, let them cook until nearly tender, then season them with salt and pepper and butter. Thicken the gravy with flour, remove and cool. Butter a pudding dish, line the sides with a rich crust. Have ready some hard-boiled eggs cut in slices. Put in a layer of egg and birds and gravy until the dish is full. Cover with a crust and bake.

BROILED PIGEONS OR SQUABS
1899

Split them down the back and broil the same as chicken; seasoning well with salt, pepper and plenty of butter. Broil slices of salt pork, very thin; place a slice over each bird and serve.

SQUIRREL

They are cooked similar to rabbits, are excellent when broiled or made into a stew, and in fact, are very good in all the different styles of cooking similar to rabbit. There are many species common to this country; among them the black, red, gray and fox. Gophers and chipmunks may also be classed as another but smaller variety.

BROILED RABBITS

After skinning and cleaning the rabbits, wipe them dry, split them down the back lengthwise, pound them flat, then wrap them in letter paper well buttered, place them on a buttered gridiron, and broil over a clear, brisk fire, turning them often. When sufficiently cooked, remove the papers, lay them on a very hot platter, season with salt, pepper and plenty of butter, turning them over and over to soak up the butter. Cover and keep hot in a warming oven until served.

BROILED VENISON STEAK
1899

Venison steaks should be boiled over a clear fire, turning often. It requires more cooking than beef. When sufficiently done, season with salt and pepper, pour over two tbsp. of currant jelly melted with a piece of butter. Serve hot on hot plates. Delicious steaks, corresponding to the shape of mutton chops, are cut from the loin.

VENISON HASHED

Cut the meat in nice small slices, and put the trimmings and bones into a saucepan with barely water enough to cover them. Let them stew for an hour. Then strain the liquid into a stew pan; add to it some bits of butter, rolled in flour, and whatever gravy was left of the venison the day before. Stir in some currant jelly, and give it a boil up. Then put in the meat, and keep it over the fire just long enough to warm it through; but do not allow it to boil, as it has been once cooked already.

BARB-B-QUE VENISON

3 or 4 lbs. meat
2 bay leaves
3 tbsp. catsup
4 tbsp. bacon drippings
2 tbsp. brown sugar
2 tbsp. salt
1 tsp. pepper
1 onion
4 tbsp. pickle juice or
2 tbsp. vinegar

Bake in moderate oven about 30 minutes per pound.

TAMALE DE CUSCELA (CORN MEAL POT PIE)
Mrs. Dr. Iglehart, 1891

One quart of corn meal scalded; add a little salt and four tbsp. of melted butter or lard. The meat may be all pork or chicken and pork mixed, boiled until tender and cut up in small pieces. Stir into the meal a double handful of flour, two beaten eggs, and onto this pour enough of the broth to make a thin batter. Take two or three large red peppers chopped fine and half can of tomatoes, beat thoroughly together and cook in a little lard or butter until well done, then put the chopped meat into the last ingredients and mix well. After this line your pie dish with the corn meal mixture, having first greased it well, and then put in the mixture in layers as for a chicken pie. Bake very slowly, and when nearly done, dress over the top with butter, put in the oven and cook until done.

HAM PIE

Pick the ham into small pieces, boil a cup of rice, beat up two eggs and stir in the ham and rice; season with pepper, salt and onion; put into a deep dish and bake.

CHILI Y HUEVOS CON CARNE
(PEPPER AND EGGS WITH MEAT)
Mrs. Dr. Iglehart, 1891

Toast the peppers in the fire, remove the seeds and cut in small pieces. Have ready some hot lard in a saucepan, into which throw a handful of chopped onions and a half a cup of can tomatoes; pour in a cup of water, and when it is boiling, put in four or more beaten eggs, stirring steadily for several minutes; put in the chopped peppers, and when on the dish ready to serve, cover the whole with grated cheese. This is truly delicious.

CHILI REYENES (STUFFED PEPPERS)
Mrs. Dr. Iglehart, 1891

Take a dozen large green peppers, toast them in the fire, slit carefully down one side and remove the seeds. Take boiled meat of any kind, that is minced as fine as possible; a few cooked onions, minced; one can tomatoes, leaving out the juice that is in it; a little cinnamon, a little powdered cloves, a few currants, and one boiled egg, all made into a paste. Take the slit peppers, stuff them with the mass and close carefully, wrapping with a thread. Beat four eggs, whites and yellows separately, put them together, dip each pepper in, and fry in a large quantity of boiling lard until quite brown.

Sauces and Dressings

DRAWN BUTTER
1899

Melted butter is the foundation of most of the common sauces. Have a covered saucepan for this purpose. One lined with porcelain will be best. Take a quarter of a pound of best fresh butter, cut it up, and mix with it about one tbsp. of flour. When it is thoroughly mixed, put it into the saucepan and set it in a large tin pan of boiling water. Shake it round continually (always moving it the same way) till it is entirely melted and begins to simmer. Then let it rest till it boils up. If you set it on too hot a fire it will be oily. If the butter and flour are not well mixed, it will be lumpy. If you put in too much water, it will be thin and poor. All these defects are to be carefully avoided.

In melting butter for sweet or pudding sauce, you may use milk instead of water.

EGG SAUCE, OR WHITE SAUCE

Mix two tbsp. of sifted flour with half a teacup of warm butter. Place over the fire a saucepan containing a pint of sweet milk and a saltspoon of salt, and a dash of white pepper; when it reaches the boiling point, add the butter and flour, stirring briskly until it thickens and becomes like cream. Have ready three cold hard-boiled eggs, sliced and chopped, add them to the sauce; let them heat through thoroughly, and serve in a boat. If you have plenty of cream, use it and omit the butter. By omitting the eggs, you have the same as "White sauce."

ONION SAUCE

Work together until light a heaping tbsp. of flour and half a cupful of butter, and gradually add two cups of boiling milk; stir constantly until it comes to a boil; then stir into that, four tender boiled onions that have been chopped fine. Salt and pepper to taste. Serve with boiled veal, poultry or mutton.

TEXAS TOMATO CATSUP

To one gallon strained tomatoes put one quart vinegar, one large cup sugar, four tbsp. each of pepper, mustard, salt, mixed spices, one tsp. red pepper. Boil until thick and then strain again. Large red peppers and onions may be added; keep tasting until it tastes good.

MINT SAUCE

Take fresh young spearmint leaves stripped from the stems; wash and drain them, or dry on a cloth. Chop very fine, put in a gravy boat, and to three tbsp. of mint put two of white sugar; mix and let it stand a few minutes, then pour over it six tbsp. of good cider or white-wine vinegar. The sauce should be made some time before it is to be used, so that the flavor of the mint may be well extracted. Fine with roast lamb.

SHARP BROWN SAUCE

Put in a saucepan one tbsp. of chopped onion, three tbsp. of good cider vinegar, six tbsp. of water, three of tomato catsup, a little pepper and salt, half a cup of melted butter, in which stir a tbsp. of sifted flour; put all together and boil until it thickens. This is most excellent with boiled meats, fish and poultry.

WINE SAUCE FOR GAME
1898

Half a glass of currant jelly, half a glass of port wine, half a glass of water, a tbsp. of cold butter, a tsp. of salt, the juice of half a lemon, a pinch of cayenne pepper and three cloves. Simmer all together a few minutes, adding the wine after it is strained. A few spoonfuls of the gravy from the game may be added to it. This sauce is especially nice with venison.

BRANDY OR WINE SAUCE

Take one cupful of butter, two of powdered sugar, the whites of two eggs, five tbsp. of sherry wine or brandy and a quarter of a cupful of boiling water. Beat butter and sugar to a cream, add the whites of the eggs, one at a time, unbeaten, and then the wine or brandy. Place the bowl in hot water and stir till smooth and frothy.

CURRANT JELLY SAUCE

Three tbps. of butter, one onion, one bay leaf, one sprig of celery, two tbsp. of vinegar, half a cupful of currant jelly, one tbsp. of flour, one pint of stock, salt, pepper. Cook the butter and onion until the latter begins to color. Add the flour and herbs. Stir until brown; add the stock, and simmer twenty minutes. Strain and skim off all the fat. Add the jelly and stir over the fire until it is melted. Serve with game.

CIDER APPLE SAUCE

Boil four quarts of new cider until it is reduced to two quarts; then put into it enough pared and quartered apples to fill the kettle; let the whole stew over a moderate fire four hours; add cinnamon if liked. This sauce is very fine with almost any kind of meat.

SAUCE PIQUANTE
ca. 1901

2 onions	2 Pickles, 2 inches in Length
1 tbsp. Butter	1 tbsp. of Strong French Vinegar
2 cloves of garlic	
1 sprig each of thyme, parsley and bay leaf	Salt and pepper to taste
	Cayenne or Hot Pepper

Chop two onions very fine. Smother in a tbsp. of butter. When well cooked, without burning, add one tbsp. of consommé or water. Add two cloves of garlic, minced very fine, and the herbs minced very fine. Season to taste with hot pepper. Take two pickles about two inches in length, and cut into thin slices of about a quarter of an inch in thickness. Put this into the sauce, with a tsp. of strong vinegar, and let the whole boil about five minutes. Serve with boiled beef, boiled beef tongue, boiled pork tongue, or any boiled meats.

TO DRESS CURRY (BOMBAY)
Mrs. I. A. Staniforth, 1891

Take two large cooking apples, four onions, one and a half lbs. mutton or fowl, cut into pieces about the size of a mouthful, one-fourth lb. of fresh butter, one teacupful of sour cream, one tbsp. of curry powder. First melt the butter in a frying pan, taking care not to burn it, then add the onions and mix them well with the butter, stirring together for ten minutes; then add the sour cream and curry powder, stirring them together for ten minutes; then add the apples, stirring them well together in the frying pan, then transfer the whole to a saucepan with a close fitting lid, rinsing the frying pan with a little boiling water. Let all stew for three hours and just before serving add salt, the juice of half a lemon and a large tsp. of chutney; a slice of pounded coconut may be substituted for half the quantity of cream.

Dumplings

SWEDISH DUMPLINGS
Great Grandma Ray

2 eggs beat slightly, add ¾ or ⅔ cup of milk, 1 tsp. salt, and add flour until stiff dough that can be handled. Roll out and cut into strips and drop into hot chicken broth and cook; at least 1 hour. Cook longer if necessary. Add 1 cup of milk and bring to a boil just before serving add 1 tbsp. of butter. Serve with chicken.

SAUERKRAUT AND DUMPLINGS
Dorothea Harms Hornburg, 1845

In a pot fry till crisp 3 strips of bacon, remove and put aside the bacon strips. Add to bacon grease 2 cups of sauerkraut (rinsed in water) and crumble in bacon strips. Cover with water, bring to boil, drop dumpling dough in. Cook uncovered 10 minutes then cover and cook 10 minutes longer.

Dumplings:
1½ cups flour
2 tsp. baking powder
A tip of salt to ¾ tsp.

1 tbsp. lard
¾ cup milk or less
1 egg

Knead to dough

NEVER FAIL CHICKEN AND DUMPLINGS
1899

2½ cups flour	½ tsp. pepper
1 tsp. baking powder	½ cup shortening
½ tsp. salt	Milk

Sift flour, baking powder, salt and pepper together. Then cut in shortening. Add enough milk for stiff dough. Roll out on floured board and cut in pieces. Drop the dumplings into boiling chicken broth. When all the dumplings have been dropped into the broth, put a tight fitting lid on the pot and let them cook for approximately 15 minutes. DO NOT PEEK (this is the secret if you do they will all fall apart).

APPLE DUMPLINGS
Mrs. I. V. Davis, 1891

To one quart flour sift tsp. soda and add half tsp. salt; lard the size of two hen's eggs; rub well together and work in enough sour or buttermilk to make a soft dough. Roll and cut size of saucer. Peel and slice half dozen large apples and add two teacups sugar and half teacup of water; let boil five minutes and put the fruit on the dough, bring the edges together over fruit and place in a greased deep pan; pour liquid from boiled apples over; slice butter the size of a hen's egg over, and add one teacup sugar and two of water; grate nutmeg over surface, and bake in an oven not very hot, for one and a half hours.

Salads and Salad Dressings

☆ ☆ ☆

BE NOT WASTEFUL

To know how to cook economically is an art. Making money is an art. Now, is there not more money made and lost in the kitchen than almost any where else? Does not many a hardworking man have his substance wasted in the kitchen? A careless cook can waste as much as a man can earn, which might as well be saved.

☆ ☆ ☆

LAMBS QUARTER WEED AND KERLIS WEED

Lambs Quarter weed and Kerlis weed were also used as a very special vegetable in the Republic of Texas. Gather the green shoots and leaves in the spring. Wash and boil in large pot for 15 minutes — drain liquid, rinse add more water, boil another 15 minutes. Drain, rinse and add more water barely covering the greens, salt to taste and add 2 tbsp. of bacon grease to each two quarts of greens. This is considered a great delicacy. Serve with hot crackling bread.

SOUTHERN AMBROSIA SALAD

3 large grapefruit, sectioned
4 large oranges, peeled and sliced
4 bananas, peeled and sliced
¾ cup flaked coconut
⅓ cup of sugar

Layer grapefruit sections, orange slices and bananas in bowl, sprinkle each layer with coconut and sugar. To section grapefruit, cut slice from top, cut off peel round and round, spiral fashion, cutting deep enough to remove white membrane. Cut along each section, dividing membrane from outside to core, remove section by section over bowl to save juice. Top with whipped cream.

TANTE SIDA'S SALAD DRESSING

Tante Sida (Mrs. Henry Streuer) was a good cook and loved having large family dinners.

3 eggs
1 cup sugar
½ cup water
½ cup milk
1 tbsp. vinegar or lemon juice
½ cup heavy cream whipped

Beat the eggs thoroughly, add sugar gradually, then add water and milk. Cook over low heat or in a double boiler until thick. Be sure to stir mixture constantly. Cool and then chill. About an hour before serving add the vinegar or lemon juice and whipped cream. Tante Sida used this on her waldorf salad, but it is excellent on any mixture of fruits.

MARGARET STILES' SALAD DRESSING

One scant tbsp. sugar; one scant tbsp. mustard; one scant tbsp. corn starch; three well beaten eggs; one cup sweet milk; one cup not too strong vinegar; pinch of salt.

Dissolve mustard in a little vinegar, mix all together, boil in double boiler until thick and while yet warm, add butter the size of an egg.

MAYONNAISE DRESSING

Put the yolks of four fresh raw eggs, with two hard-boiled ones, into a cold bowl. Rub these as smooth as possible before introducing the oil; a good measure of oil is a tbsp. to each yolk of raw egg. All the art consists in introducing the oil by degrees, a few drops at a time. You can never make a good salad without taking plenty of time. When the oil is well mixed, and assumes the appearance of jelly, put in two heaping tsp. of dry table salt, one of pepper and one of made mustard. Never put in salt and pepper before this stage of the process, because the salt and pepper would coagulate the albumen of the eggs, and you could not get the dressing smooth. Two tbsp. of vinegar added gradually.

The Mayonnaise should be the thickness of thick cream when finished, but if it looks like curdling when mixing it, set in a cold place for about forty minutes or an hour, then mix it again. It is a good idea to place it in a pan of cracked ice while mixing.

Salad dressing should be kept in a separate bowl in a cold place and not mixed with the salad until the moment it is to be served, or it may lose its crispness and freshness.

DRESSING FOR COLD SLAW
1899

Beat up two eggs with two tbsp. of sugar, add a piece of butter the size of half an egg, a tsp. of mustard, a little pepper, and lastly a teacup of vinegar. Put all of these ingredients into a dish over the fire and cook like a soft custard. Some think it improved by adding half a cupful of thick sweet cream to this dressing; in that case use less vinegar. Either way is very fine.

MRS. GEORGE HUME'S CREAM DRESSING FOR COLD SLAW
1891

Two tbsp. of whipped cream, two of sugar, four of vinegar. Beat well and pour over cabbage previously cut very fine and seasoned with salt.

SALAD DRESSING FOR LETTUCE
Mrs. Tallichet, 1891

To the yolk of one hard boiled egg, rubbed smooth, add one anchovy, one mustard spoon of Dusseldorfer mustard, two tbsp. of olive oil, a little salt and pepper and one tbsp. of best vinegar. The lettuce is better torn in small pieces and the dressing added by each person immediately before eating.

TUNA SALAD

1 cup white tuna	1 cup celery
3 hard boiled eggs	1 cup nuts
2 apples	Mayonnaise

CUCUMBER SALAD
1901

2 fine cucumbers   A plain French dressing.

Wash and slice two nice young cucumbers, and use a plain dressing of vinegar, salt and pepper. This is a very delicious salad. There are many so-called elegant novelties introduced lately in the way of serving cucumbers, such as stuffed cucumbers, fried cucumbers, etc. The Creoles look with disdain, and justly, on these silly innovations in the serving of a vegetable which nature intended to be used for salad purposes and nothing else.

DANDELION SALAD

1 pint of fresh white dandelion   A plain French dressing

Cut off the roots and green portion of the leaves, wash and steep in salt and water. When they become crisp, drain and press dry, rub the salad bowl with a clove of garlic and season the dandelions with French dressing. This salad may also be served with two hard-boiled eggs cut in quarters or sliced and laid over or with two medium-sized beets, sliced, and seasoned with a plain French dressing.

CHICKEN SALAD

Boil the fowls tender and remove all the fat, gristle and skin; mince the meat in small pieces, but do not hash it. To one chicken put twice and a half its weight in celery, cut in pieces of about one-quarter of an inch; mix thoroughly and set it in a cold place.

In the meantime prepare a "Mayonnaise dressing," and when ready for the table pour this dressing over the chicken and celery, tossing and mixing it thoroughly. Set it in a cool place until ready to serve. Garnish with celery tips, or cold hard-boiled eggs, lettuce leaves, from the heart, and cold boiled beets.

Crisp cabbage is a good substitute for celery; when celery is not to be had, use celery vinegar in the dressing. Turkey makes a fine salad.

MIXED SUMMER SALAD

Three heads of lettuce, two tsp. of green mustard leaves, a handful of water cress's, five tender radishes, one cucumber, three hard-boiled eggs, two tsp. of white sugar, one tsp. of salt, one tsp. of pepper, one tsp. of made mustard, one teacupful of vinegar, half a teacupful of oil.

Mix all well together.

ORANGE AND BANANA SALAD
ca. 1885

Peel oranges removing all white skin. Cut in ¼-inch slices. Place two slices on each lettuce covered plates. Cover with two length wise quarters of banana which have been covered in lemon juice and rolled on ground nuts.

Top with sliced oranges, garnish with mayonnaise and maraschino cherries.

HAM SALAD

Take cold boiled ham, fat and lean together, chop it until it is thoroughly mixed and the pieces are about the size of peas; then add to this an equal quantity of celery cut fine, if celery is out of season, lettuce may be substituted. Line a dish thickly with lettuce leaves and fill with the chopped ham and celery. Make a dressing the same as for cold slaw and turn over the whole. Very fine.

PIMENTO SALAD
Margaret Stiles, ca. 1885

One cup chopped apples; one cup chopped celery; one cup chopped almonds; one cup chopped walnuts; juice of three small lemons with water enough to fill a cup; one cup sugar; one tsp. salt; one box gelatin; four pimentoes.

Mix thoroughly and set on ice. Serve with mayonnaise with lettuce leaf.

MARGARET STILES' MAYONNAISE

Yolks of three eggs beaten stiff, beat ¾ cup of Wesson's Cooking Oil into the eggs one drop at a time. Season with ½ tsp. salt, red pepper and juice of one lemon. Put on ice until ready to serve.

POTATO SALAD, HOT

Pare six or eight large potatoes, boil till done and slice thin while hot; peel and cut up three large onions into small bits and mix with the potatoes; cut up some breakfast bacon into small bits, sufficient to fill a teacup and fry it a light brown; remove the meat, and into the grease stir three tbsp. of vinegar, making a sour gravy, which with the bacon pour over the potato and onion; mix lightly. To be eaten when hot.

Vegetables and Pasta

SPAETZLE

Noodles and Spaetzle are always German favorites. When our father came to dinner at our house his request was for anything, so long as there were noodles or Spaetzle and gravy.

1 egg per person   **1 tbsp. luke warm water**

Add enough flour and a little salt to make a firm dough. Cook in a large pot of boiling, salted water (a spaghetti cooker works well). Before putting dough in a spaetzle press, dip press in boiling water — then fill press ¾ full and press into boiling salted water. Cook about a minute or two until spaetzle rises to top. Lift spaetzle out of water with spaghetti cooker basket or any strainer and put in another pot. Sprinkle lightly with melted butter, stir and keep on very low heat until all are cooked and ready to serve. Serve with gravy or browned butter with bread crumbs. If a press is not available the dough can be rolled or patted on a floured board and cut in small pieces or strips.

NOODLES

4 eggs　　　　　　　　　　Flour
2 tbsp. milk

Beat the eggs, add milk, and the flour, using enough to make a dough that is easy to handle — not sticky. Roll dough very thin on a floured board. Put a clean towel over a chair back and lay the dough on the towel to dry until it is slightly hard. When the dough is dry enough, roll it up like a jelly roll and cut into thin or wider strips, as desired. Separate strips and place on a cookie sheet to dry some more. Noodles can be made the day before using. Cook in boiling salted water until just tender. Serve with gravy or browned butter and bread crumbs.

TEXAS OKRA AND TOMATOES

Take an equal quantity of each, let the okra be young, slice it, skin the tomatoes; put them into a pan without water, add a lump of butter, an onion chopped fine, some pepper and salt; stew them one hour.

STUFFED CABBAGE (GEFULLTE KOHL)

Mrs. Julius Streuer and Mrs. Wm. Streuer

This dish was always served for holidays and special occasion dinners.

1 lb. ground round steak
1 to 2 tbsp. shortening
Salt and pepper to taste
1 large head cabbage
½ cup butter, browned

6 slices dry bread, preferably homemade
3 large eggs, slightly beaten
¼ tsp. nutmeg

Fry ground meat with just a little fat. Season with salt and pepper to taste. Set aside. Take cabbage head and cut so the outer leaves will be left intact for the stuffing to put inside. Use about 6 to 7 leaves. Cut the rest of the cabbage coarsely and cook in salted water until tender, drain well and reserve liquid. Soak bread in water and squeeze dry as possible (leave bread in water just long enough to moisten well). Mix eggs well with the bread, drained cabbage and the meat. Add the nutmeg and taste to check seasoning. Add more salt and nutmeg to your taste. Keep warm.

Hang a piece of cheese cloth, muslin or a soft kitchen towel (flour sack variety) over a colander and place outside cabbage leaves inside the cloth. Put the hot filling (it must be hot) in the large cabbage leaves. Fold leaves over filling to resemble a cabbage head, then tie up cloth. Place reserved cabbage liquid in a large kettle; place cabbage in boiling liquid, add more water if necessary. Cover and cook over medium heat for 1 hour. Take cabbage out and drain in colander. Squeeze a little, if necessary to get liquid out. Remove cloth. Place cabbage in a large bowl and pour browned butter over the top.

TOMATO BELL

Mattie Smith Kirkland, c. 1879

- 2 large green tomatoes
- 4 bell peppers
- 1 hot pepper
- 6 apples (not peeled)
- 2 red peppers
- 5 onions

Grind above ingredients together. Drain juice off. Add one cup sugar and 1 cup vinegar. Tie in a cloth 1 tsp. cinnamon, 1 tsp. cloves, and 1 tsp. all spice. Add to above ingredients and bring to a hard boil. Boil for ten minutes. Pour into sterilized jars and seal.

TOMATOES AND CREAM

Pare and slice ripe tomatoes; one pound of fresh ones; stew until perfectly smooth, season with salt and pepper, and add a piece of butter the size of an egg. Just before taking from the fire, stir in cup of cream, with a tbsp. of flour stirred smooth in a part of it; do not let it boil after the flour is put in. Have ready in a dish some pieces of toast; pour the tomatoes over this.

BAKED BEANS
1900

Nora Scott Rogers fed these beans to the prisoners in the jail as well as the homeless people who camped on the banks of the Llano River many times. She was a caring and giving person. Her husband W. T. Rogers served as Sheriff of Llano County, Texas, in the early 1900s. (This recipe serves 50)

8 lbs. beans, soaked overnight, drain and add:

4 lbs. salt pork	3 to 4 tbsp. prepared mustard
4 qts. tomato juice	3 large onions, chopped fine
1 tsp. minced garlic	3 cup molasses

Bake in moderate oven.

CHILI BEANS
"An elderly lady in Rockport, TX"

3 lbs. dry pintos	2 onions
Garlic	5 tbsp. salt – 5 cloves
Jalapenos (mild) about nine oz.	8-quart kettle

Get up early, pick and wash beans and cook slowly several hours until beans are nearly done. Then – lightly brown three pounds ground round steak.

2 onions	3 tsp. chili powder
2 cloves garlic	Salt to taste (allow for salt on
4 oz. tomato paste	crackers

Mix with beans, just before serving break in saltines to thicken enough. *Note:* 2 lbs. beans and meat serves 30. 6 ozs. hot jalapenos, juice and all, for 4 lbs. of meat and beans. Serves 30 to 40.

GREAT GRANDMOTHER'S BAKED BEANS

1 quart dry beans (4 cups)
1 lb. bacon
2 tbsp. sorgum molasses
1 tsp. soda
Salt to taste

Wash the beans in hot water, drain, put in kettle with the bacon and cover with boiling water; boil half an hour. Add the soda, stir well, cook 5 minutes and skim into a bean pot. Season with salt, add the molasses. Score the rind of the bacon, cover it with the beans, add boiling water until it stands on the top, and place it in a moderate oven. Bake steadily for six hours, adding hot water as they dry. After that time cover may be left off, and the beans baked as dry as liked. The secret of success lies in using hot water throughout; cold water hardens and toughens beans. The bacon is much nicer than salt pork, giving a delicate smoky flavor. This recipe makes 4 quarts when done.

FRIED SQUASH

1900

Take a bunch of freshly picked squash, cut the squash into thin slices and sprinkle with salt. Let the squash stand a few minutes. Beat 2 eggs and dip the squash into egg and fry until brown in butter.

BOILED LEEKS

Trim off the coarser leaves of young leeks, cut them into equal lengths, tie them in small bunches, and boil in plenty of water, previously salted. Serve on toast, and send melted butter to the table with them.

CARROTS AND CORN

6 young carrots
Cream or milk
6 ears of corn

Butter
Seasoning

Scrub and dice carrots, cover with salt water, and set over fire. While carrots are cooking, prepare the corn. Scrape off the kernels with the back of a silver knife. Be sure to get all the milk that is in the corn. When carrots are nearly done, turn corn into them without emptying the water in which they are cooking. Add cream and butter until you have enough liquor, sprinkle with seasoning and cook 5 minutes, when the corn should be done.

SAUERKRAUT

A very special recipe that could be carried on the wagon train.

Gather the cabbage and take off the outside leaves, wash and quarter them, take out the core, and put in a clean barrel until there are enough to cut well. Then with a clean, sharp spade, cut them fine and sprinkle with a little salt. One quart of salt is enough for forty gallons of Kraut. If too much is put in, it will not sour. Pound until water rises; add more cabbage and proceed as before, then take large cabbage leaves, wash, cover the Kraut with them, and put on a board, with a stone for a weight, wash the board and stone once a week until the Kraut has ceased fermenting. Be sure to keep enough water on it to cover it, or the Kraut will spoil. If made in cool weather, keep it in a warm place until sour enough to suit the taste.

[A historic recipe, please check with dietitian before eating.]

TO COOK RICE SO THAT ITS GRAINS WILL STAND ALONE
Mrs. Charles Raymond, 1891

Wash until the water is clear, then boil fifteen minutes (put in boiling water), strain, and place covered saucepan on the back of stove to steam for fifteen minutes, when the grains will crack open and be tender.

BAKED CAULIFLOWER
Margaret Youngblood Stiles, 1885

Cook one large or 2 small heads of cauliflower in salt and water until tender. Run through colander. Mix in 3 well-beaten eggs and 1 cup cream sauce. Pour in buttered dish and bake a few minutes, or long enough to set. Then turn out on a flat dish and serve, covering each serving with hot cream sauce to which has been added minced boiled ham.

STEWED CELERY
Great-Grandmother Beulah Harding Hancock Hayne

Wash, scrape, and cut stalks crosswise. Place in a stew pan and barely cover with hot water. Add ½ tsp. salt for every pint of celery. Cook until tender—about 30 minutes. Use liquid that is left for making sauce. If not enough, add milk.

Sauce: ½ cup liquid for each pint of celery, ⅔ tbsp. butter, ⅔ tbsp. flour, ¼ tsp. salt, melt butter, add flour and salt. When smooth, add liquid and cook until thick as desired.

BUTTERED ONIONS

For each onion add ½ tsp. of butter, ⅛ tsp. salt, a few grains of pepper. Peel and quarter onions, place in boiling water. Boil 5 minutes, drain, add more boiling water. When the onions are tender, drain again and add seasoning.

FRIED OKRA

Place okra pods in cold water to which salt has been added. Let boil until tender enough to pierce with fork. Take from the water, roll in corn meal and fry in plenty of hot fat until crisp and brown.

HOMINY

Soak ½ gal. white corn overnight. Add 2 tbsp. of soda at morning and put on to cook. Cook till eyes (of corn) slip, then wash good and cook in fresh water until tender. If water in second boiling is very yellow, drain off and add fresh water.

POTATO PUFFS

Prepare the potatoes as for mashed potato. While hot, shape in balls about the size of an egg. Have a tin sheet well buttered and place the balls on it. As soon as all are done, brush over with beaten egg. Brown.

BAKED SWEET POTATOES

Wash and scrape them, split them lengthwise. Steam or boil them until nearly done. Drain, and put them in a baking dish, placing over them lumps of butter, pepper and salt; sprinkle thickly with sugar, and bake in the oven to a nice brown.

Hubbard squash is nice cooked in the same manner.

A GOOD RECIPE FOR POOR SWEET POTATOES

Mrs. Littlefield, 1891

Peel, slice, and place in crock or pan; two or three spoonfuls of butter and half cup of sugar and cup of water poured over, cook until a nice light brown.

OYSTERETTES

Margaret Stiles, 1885

1 cup cold mashed Irish potatoes   2 eggs beaten well
1 cup cold meat chopped fine

Season with salt and pepper and mix thoroughly. Drop by spoonfuls in hot grease and fry a nice brown.

ONIONS BAKED

Use a large onion, the best for this purpose; wash them clean, but do not peel, and put into a saucepan with slightly salted water; boil an hour, replacing the water with more boiling hot as it evaporates; turn off the water and lay the onions on a cloth to dry them well; roll each one in a piece of buttered tissue paper, twisting it at the top to keep it on and bake in a slow oven about an hour, or until tender all through; peel them; place in a deep dish and brown slightly, basting well with butter for fifteen minutes; season with salt and pepper and pour some melted butter over them.

FRIED CUCUMBERS

Pare them and cut lengthwise in very thick slices; wipe them dry with a cloth; sprinkle with salt and pepper, dredge with flour, and fry in lard and butter, a tbsp. of each mixed. Brown both sides and serve warm.

CORN PUDDING

Scrape the substance out of twelve ears of tender, green, uncooked corn (it is better scraped than grated, as you do not get those husky particles which you cannot avoid with a grater); add yolks and whites, beaten separately, of four eggs, a tsp. of sugar the same of flour mixed in a tbsp. of butter, a small quantity of salt and pepper, and one pint of milk. Bake about half or three-quarters of an hour.

FRIED EGG-PLANT

Take fresh, purple egg-plants of a middling size; cut them in slices a quarter of an inch thick, and soak them for half an hour in cold water, with a tsp. of salt in it. Have ready some cracker or bread crumbs and one beaten egg; drain off the water from the slices, lay them on a napkin, dip them in the crumbs and then in the egg, put another coat of crumbs on them and fry them in butter to a light brown. The frying pan must be hot before the slices are put in — they will fry in ten minutes.

You may pare them before you put them into the frying pan, or you may pull off the skins when you take them up. You must not remove them from the water until you are ready to cook them, as the air will turn them black.

CHOP SUEY

Margaret Stiles, 1885

Boil one cup of rice until well done. Fry one pound of hamburger steak and 2 or 3 onions until brown. Turn rice meat and onions into a good sized baking dish, moisten with 2 cups of cooked tomatoes. Season well with salt, pepper and large spoonful of butter. Pimentos may be added if flavor is liked. Bake for two hours while keeping mixture well stirred.

Cakes

WEDDING CAKE
Republic of Texas

President Lamar, entrusting his Commissioners Five, a Capitol Site to secure,
Undertaking this, they reached the Colorado River and Austin fair,
And at once did select. They looked the Vista over
And everywhere saw trees,
Interspersed with violet shadows, that here did please.
Of people, they took note of families three,
One Jacob Harrell, a merchant worthy;
Another from Montopolis was,
While the other was a William Barton and his daughter.
I will now try to enlighten.

Early Cupid had played a part in these two young people's lives,
And the young man thought he was choosing the best of wives.
Plans for a real wedding with an affair thereafter, see;
Game and other good things could provided be.
But whence was the flour for the wedding cake to come?
What, no wedding cake? The neighborhoods were searched one and all,
But no flour could be found,
Then to Bastrop to search one did go.
But came back empty handed with a NO.

Then ingenuity was ready to do her best.
Of course it was a woman that made the test;
She sifted the corn meal many times and well.
That's not so easy to believe as to tell.
Then she had ready and clean her Red Flannel Balmoral,
And through it sifted the sifted corn meal, and that's all.
Presto, FLOUR.
And then she did make a Bride's cake,
What won't a woman do for friendship's sake?
So good it was, it would make one squeal.
Just think of it, a Bride's cake made of corn meal!
Days of feasting and having dinners great,
Were wedding customs of that time and date.
This is claimed to be the very first wedding cake in Austin fair.
But Weddings cause trouble to some one, all the time, everywhere.

CHOCOLATE POTATO CAKE

1 cup butter
2 cups sugar
4 eggs
3 oz. unsweetened chocolate melted
1 cup cold mashed potatoes
2 cups sifted flour
1 tsp. baking soda
1 tsp. cinnamon
¼ tsp. nutmeg
1 cup buttermilk.
1 cup pecans, chopped

Cream the butter and add the sugar and beat until mixture is light and fluffy. Add the eggs and beat well. Stir in the potatoes and melted chocolate. Mix well. Sift together the flour, soda, cinnamon and nutmeg. Add alternately to the creamed mixture with the buttermilk. Mix well. Stir in the pecans. Pour batter in a greased and bread crumb (dry) dusted tube pan. Bake in moderate oven about 45 minutes. Cool in pan for 15 minutes and then turn out and cool on rack. Dust cake with powdered sugar before serving or frost with Deluxe Chocolate Fudge Frosting or Chocolate Butter Frosting.

DELUXE CHOCOLATE FUDGE FROSTING

1 cup sugar
3 tbsp. cornstarch
3 tbsp. cocoa
1 cup boiling water
3 tbsp. butter
1 tsp. vanilla

In a saucepan, combine the sugar, cornstarch and cocoa. Stir well to blend. Add boiling water and stir while cooking over low heat until thick. Remove from heat and add butter and vanilla. Mix well. Spread on cooled cake while icing is still hot.

KATE HURT'S POTATO CAKE

1 cup shortening
4 cups flour
1 tbsp. cocoa
2 tbsp. cinnamon
1 cup cherries
2 cups sugar
¾ cup milk
2 tsp. baking powder
1 tsp. all spice
1 cup pecans
1 cup raisins

Stir in beaten egg whites last. Cook in moderate oven about one hour.

OMA STREUER'S NUSS TORTE (NUT CAKE)

1 cup butter
2 cups sugar
3 cups sifted flour
3 tsp. baking powder
1 cup milk
2 cups ground pecans
2 tsp. vanilla
8 egg whites, stiffly beaten

Cream together the butter and sugar; add the dry ingredients, which have been sifted together, alternately with the milk. Stir in the pecans and vanilla. Gently fold in the stiffly beaten egg whites. Bake in a greased and floured tube pan in a moderate oven for 1 hour and 30 minutes or until done. Cool in pan 15 minutes, then finish cooling on a rack. Frost with powdered sugar icing and decorate with whole pecans.

POWDERED SUGAR ICING FOR NUSS TORTE

Marie Klein Streuer made Nuss Torte cake for all special occasions.

1 lb. powdered sugar, sifted
4 or 5 tbsp. butter, melted

Sweet cream
1 tsp. vanilla

Add the butter to the powdered sugar and add enough cream to make a thick creamy icing. Stir in vanilla. The icing will be soft and creamy if kept over hot water while mixing.

CHOCOLATE BUTTER FROSTING

½ cup butter or margarine
1 lb. confectioners sugar
⅛ tsp. salt
1 egg yolk

3 oz. melted unsweetened chocolate
4 to 5 tbsp. hot water
1½ tsp. vanilla

Cream the butter and sugar until well blended. Add the egg yolk and salt. Beat well. Add the chocolate and beat well. Add the water gradually—just enough to give a good spreading consistency. Beat well. Add vanilla and mix well. Spread on cooled cake. *Note:* ⅔ cup to ¾ cup cocoa may be substituted for chocolate and sift cocoa with sugar.

POOR MAN'S CAKE

Arinda Standifer Wolf

1 cup water
⅓ cup lard
1 cup sugar

1 cup raisins
1 tsp. cinnamon
½ teaspoon nutmeg

Boil all together for 3 minutes, cool. Add: 2 cups flour sifted, ½ tsp. soda, 1 tsp. baking powder, ½ tsp. salt, ½ cup nutmeat.

MAMA'S GROUND PECAN CAKE

1½ cups flour
1 cup sugar
½ cup butter
½ cup milk

4 egg whites, beaten stiff
2 heaping teaspoons baking powder
Vanilla

Cream butter and sugar until light and fluffy. Add milk, vanilla, flour and baking powder, a little at a time. Fold in stiff egg whites. Pour into three greased and floured cake pans. Bake in a moderate oven for 25 to 30 minutes.

Pecan Filling:

3 cups ground pecans
⅔ cup sugar
2 eggs
1 tbsp. butter

1 cup sour cream
1 tbsp. lemon juice
  and grated rind

Put sugar, eggs, butter, cream and flour into a saucepan over low heat. Stir constantly until thick. Add ground pecans, lemon juice and rind. Spread between layers and on top of cake.

THE GOBLET CAKE

To be measured in a large goblet.

¾ goblet of butter
2 goblets of sugar
⅔ goblet of sweet milk

3 goblets of flour
1 tsp. of baking powder
Whites of 8 eggs

Take one-half the flour and cream with butter; add baking powder to the other half of the flour, and sift in last thing with the milk. Beat whites to a stiff froth and add the sugar; but all together, beat well and flavor. Bake as loaf or layer cake.

FEATHER CAKE

2 cups sugar
½ cup butter
1 cup sweet milk
Whites of 3 eggs

3 cups flour
2½ tsp. baking powder
Vanilla

Sift sugar and flour separately several times. Measure out ½ cup flour and set aside. Then sift the baking powder with the remaining 2½ cups flour. Cream sugar and butter. If it does not cream readily mix a little of milk with it. Add flour and milk and eggs, last of all flavor to taste. Bake in moderate oven about 30 minutes.

CAKE OF 1846
Very old recipe!

1 cup butter	1 cup milk
2 cups sugar	Pinch of salt
4 eggs	3 tsp. baking powder
3 cups flour	Vanilla

Sift flour, baking powder and salt. Mix butter, sugar, eggs and milk; mix in flour mixture, add vanilla — makes 4 layers. This cake may be iced with chocolate, lemon, coconut, pineapple — whatever is desired.

GREAT-GRANDMOTHER KINCAID'S FAVORITE WHITE CAKE
Temperance Rattan Kincaid

¾ cup butter (or ⅔ cup lard)	2 level tsp. baking powder
2 cups sugar	5 egg whites beaten stiff
2½ cups flour	1 tsp. vanilla
1 cup sweet milk	

Cream butter or lard and sugar, sift flour and measure, then add baking powder and sift 3 or 4 times. Add milk and flour alternately to sugar and butter mixture. Lastly fold in beaten egg whites. Add vanilla. Bake in two layers or as a loaf cake. Use any kind of filling as desired.

GREAT-GRANDMOTHER'S MARBLE CAKE

⅞ cup butter	2 tbsp. cocoa
2 cups sugar	1 tsp. cinnamon
3 cups cake flour, sifted	¼ tsp. cloves
2 tsp. baking powder	¼ tsp. ginger
4 eggs	¼ tsp. nutmeg
1 cup milk	¼ tsp. allspice
1½ tsp. vanilla	

Cream butter and sugar. To creamed mixture add 1 tbsp. flour alternately with 1 egg, mixing well after each addition. Continue until all eggs are used. Stir vanilla into milk. Add remaining flour and baking powder alternately with milk, mixing thoroughly. Separate ⅓ of the batter into a small bowl. Add cocoa and spices and mix well. Grease and flour a tube pan. To marble, drop circles of plain batter into pan by heaping tablespoonfuls, 4 or 5. Cover the junctions of these circles with smaller spoonfuls of the spiced batter. Cover spiced circles with spoonfuls of plain batter and continue until all batter has been used. With a table knife cut a circle around the cake approximately 1 inch from the rim and cut a second circle approximately 1 inch from the tube. Now cut a scallop pattern back and forth from rim to tube continuing around the cake. Bake in moderate oven for 1 to 1¼ hours. (Take cake out when it still tests slightly moist.) May be served plain or glazed.

POUND CAKE

2 cups butter
2 cups sugar
10 eggs
4 cups flour
½ tsp. mace
2 tbsp. milk

Cream the butter and sugar, add the yolks of eggs beaten till thick, then the milk, flour, and whites of eggs. Pour into a square tin and bake an hour.

BLACK ANGEL CAKE

1 cup chocolate, grated
½ cup milk
2 cups brown sugar
1 egg yolk
1 tsp. vanilla
1 tsp. soda
½ cup butter
2 cups flour
2 eggs
2 tsp. baking powder
2 tbsp. water

Stir together in a saucepan the grated chocolate, milk, 1 cupful sugar, yolk 1 egg, and tsp. vanilla; cook slowly and cool. Take 1 cupful sugar, the butter, flour, milk, 2 eggs — cream butter and sugar with yolks of eggs; add milk, sifted flour, whites of eggs beaten stiff, beat together, then stir in the custard, lastly add the soda, dissolved in warm water. Pour into a cake pan and bake in a slow oven . This cake will keep a long time.

YELLOW ANGEL FOOD CAKE

Take one cup egg whites, saving four yolks in a separate bowl; one cup granulated sugar sifted three times; one cup flour sifted five times and measured after sifting; one level tsp. cream of tartar and one tsp. vanilla. Whip the egg yolks until creamy.

Whip the egg whites until foamy, add the cream of tartar and beat until they stick to the bowl when it is inverted. Fold in the sugar a little at a time, add the extract, fold in the flour alternately with the egg yolks. Pour into an ungreased cake pan. Bake in a slow oven for about an hour. Remove from the oven, invert pan over plate, let stand two hours or longer, then remove from pan by running a knife around the edge.

A PIONEER BIRTHDAY CAKE

This recipe was used to make a birthday cake for a little Texas girl long ago when there was no flour to be had. Corn was ground on a hand mill. The meal was carefully emptied from one sack to another, and the fine meal dust clinging to the sack was carefully shaken out on a paper. The sack was again emptied and shaken, and this process was repeated laboriously, time after time until two cups of meal dust was obtained. The rest of the ingredients were as follows:

One half cup of wild honey, one tsp. of home made soda, one wild turkey egg, one scant cup of sour milk, and a very small amount of butter. To all of which was added the two cups of meal dust.

The batter was poured into a skillet with a lid and placed over the open fire in the yard; the skillet lid was heaped with coals.

TAYLOR CAKE
Mrs. G. A. Searight, 1891

Eight eggs, three-fourths pound sugar, one quart molasses, three-fourths pound butter, one pint of sour milk, one tbsp. of soda, flour enough to thicken to drop on pans. Bake in moderate oven.

OLD TIMEY STACK CAKE

This recipe was brought from St. Joseph, Missouri, by Margarete Crawford.

4 eggs	1 tsp. vanilla
½ cup butter	¼ tsp. salt
2 cups sugar	3 tsp. baking powder
1 cup milk	4 cups flour
3 lbs. dried apples — cooked	

Cook apples — mash and sweeten, cream butter and sugar, add eggs and beat. Add milk and vanilla a little at a time with flour, salt, and baking powder. Pinch off dough and roll to ¼ inch — use plate to cut out rounds — about ten or twelve. Bake on top of stove on ungreased skillet or spider until brown — stack cakes or layers putting dried apples between each layer. Jelly or jam may be used instead of dried apples.

COCONUT CAKE

This recipe has been in the Carter family for many years.

1 level tsp. baking soda	2 cups flour
1 cup buttermilk	½ tsp. salt
¼ lb. butter at room temperature	2 tsp baking powder
1½ cups sugar	½ tsp. grated lemon rind
2 egg yolks	2 egg whites

Grease and flour 2 nine-inch cake tins — add soda to buttermilk, cream butter and sugar, add egg yolk and beat — add dry ingredients alternately with buttermilk. Stir in lemon rind. Beat egg whites and fold into batter — bake in moderate oven for 30 minutes.

Lemon Cream Filling: ¾ cup sugar, 1 cup boiling water, ½ cup coconut, 2 tbsp. cornstarch, ¼ cup lemon juice, 1 tbsp. butter. Mix sugar and cornstarch in saucepan — add boiling water and lemon juice. Stir in coconut and bring to rolling boil — reduce heat and cook 1 minute. Stir in butter and cool to room temperature, put between layers of cake. Ice cake with frosting and sprinkle with coconut.

PRUNE CAKE

Racheal Burnett came to Texas about 1824. The recipe has been passed down through four generations

- 1½ cups sugar
- 1 cup lard
- 3 eggs
- 1 cup buttermilk
- 2 cups flour
- 1 tsp. soda
- 1 tsp. cloves
- 1 tsp. allspice
- 1 tsp. cinnamon
- 1 tsp. nutmeg
- 1 tsp. salt
- 1 tsp. vanilla
- 1 cup prunes, cooked and chopped
- 1 cup pecans, chopped

Add sugar and eggs beat well, add lard beat well, sift all dry ingredients together, alternate flour mixture with buttermilk, add vanilla, prunes and chopped pecans. Bake in a moderate oven for 45 minutes. Icing: 2 cups powdered sugar, 2 tbsp. butter, add enough coffee to be able to pour icing over cake.

EGGLESS SPICE CAKE

Sara King Standifer, ca. 1850

Take 2 cups raisins and 2 cups water. Cook raisins in water, till water is half gone and mix in 1 cup lard or meat drippings, 2 cups sugar, ½ tsp. salt, 1 tbsp. soda, 4 cups flour, 1 tsp. ginger, ½ tsp. cinnamon, ½ tsp. nutmeg and nuts if you have them. Bake in moderate oven for about an hour. If you are short a spice or have peanuts, they are good. Being short a spice won't hurt the taste of your cake. Eat plain. It stays moist for a time. This recipe makes good cup cakes or drop cookies.

GRANNY GOLDEN'S SPICE CAKE

Martha Eleanor Crawford Golden, 1836–1918

- 2 cups sugar
- ¾ cup butter
- 4 eggs
- 1 cup sweet milk
- 3½ cups flour
- 3 tsp. baking powder
- 1 tsp. ground cloves
- 1 tbsp. cinnamon
- 1 tsp. nutmeg

Cream butter and sugar together until light and fluffy. Add whole eggs one at a time, beat until smooth. Add sifted dry ingredients alternately with milk, a small amount at a time. Beat after each addition.

Pour into three 9-inch square or round well-greased and floured pans. Bake in moderate oven for 25 minutes.

NUT AND DATE FILLING

- 2 cups sugar
- 1 cup milk
- 2 whole eggs
- 1 cup chopped pecans
- 1 cup chopped dates

Combine all ingredients and cook until spreading consistency

HOT MILK CAKE

- 4 eggs
- 2 cups sugar
- 2½ cups all purpose flour
- 2¼ tsp. baking powder
- 1 tsp. vanilla
- 1½ cups milk
- 10 tbsp. butter

Beat eggs until thick. Gradually add sugar, beating until mixture is light and fluffy. Combine flour and baking powder, add to batter with vanilla and beat until smooth. In a saucepan, heat milk and butter just until the butter melts, stirring occasionally. Add to batter, beat until combined. Pour into greased 9 x 13-inch pan. Bake in moderate oven for 30–35 minutes.

LOAF OR LAYER CAKE

Sarah Frances (Fannie) Malone, ca. 1845

1 cup sugar
2 tbsp. lard or butter (heaping)
2 cups flour
2 tsp. baking powder
1 egg in cup, then milk to fill
1 tsp. flavoring

Beat all real good. Bake slowly 45 minutes for loaf. If white cake is desired use two egg whites. Whipped cream for filling with corn starch beat in to hold it up is extra good.

[Note from Fannie: "I make all my cakes by this."]

☆ ☆ ☆

ECONOMY

Economy is an institute of nature and enforced by Bible precept: Gather up the fragments, that nothing be lost.

☆ ☆ ☆

POVERTY CAKE

½ cup sugar
½ cup jam or jelly
1 cup water
1 tsp. of soda dissolved in water
2 tbsp. butter
1 egg
1 pinch each spice and cinnamon
1½ cups flour (scant)
1 cup nuts and
1 cup raisins — floured
1 cake chocolate

Cherries also may be added with nuts. Bake in layers and use any good filling. This makes a small loaf cake about the size of a loaf of bread.

CARROT CAKE

1½ cups butter or lard
2 cups sugar
4 eggs
2 cups flour, heaping
2 tsp. cinnamon
1 tsp. salt
1½ tsp. soda
2 cups grated carrots

Mix until well blended, pour into 3 greased and floured cake pans. Bake in moderate oven for 20-25 minutes. Ice when cool.

GINGERBREAD WITH CHOCOLATE GLAZE

¾ cup butter
1 cup sugar
3 cups flour
1 cup dark molasses
1 cup black coffee
1 tsp. ginger
½ tsp. cloves
1 tsp. bicarbonate of soda
3 eggs

Mix the spices with the molasses. Dissolve the soda in a little boiling water and add to the coffee. Cream the butter and sugar, add the eggs, one at a time, and beat each one well. Add the molasses, then the coffee and flour, a little at a time, alternately. Bake in bread tins in a moderate oven 40 to 60 minutes, or until the cake leaves the sides of the pan.

BANANA CAKE

½ cup butter
1 cup sugar
½ cup milk
2 scant cups flour
1½ tsp. baking powder
Whites of 4 eggs
½ tsp. vanilla

Mix flour and baking powder, cream butter and sugar, add milk and flour alternately, then vanilla and beaten whites. Bake in 3 layer tins in hot oven. To boiled icing add ½ cupful finely sliced bananas and use as filling. Dust top with powdered sugar

GERANIUM CAKE

½ cup butter, 1 cup sugar, ⅔ cup water, ¼ tsp. salt, 2 cups flour, 1 tsp. baking powder, whites of 4 eggs. Mix flour, salt and baking powder. Cream butter and sugar, add alternately the water and flour, then whites of eggs, and whip hard five minutes. Line loaf pan with buttered paper and rose-geranium leaves. Bake in a moderate oven. The leaves can be pulled off with the paper.

☆   ☆   ☆

BAKING ADVICE

*Make the oven the right heat, and give it **time** to bake through, is the true plan; if you attempt to hurry it, you only **burn** instead of cooking it **done**.*

☆   ☆   ☆

LEMON QUEEN CAKE

2 cups sugar, 2 cups flour, 1 cup butter, 8 eggs, 2 lemons, ½ tsp. soda, ½ tsp. salt. Mix salt and soda with flour; beat butter to a light cream, and add lemon rind; beat half the sugar into it; beat yolks of eggs, then whites, then both together; add sugar to the eggs and beat well; put in lemon juice last; bake in small cake tin.

WHITE FRUIT CAKE

¾ cup butter
1½ cups sugar
3 eggs
2½ cups baking powder
½ cup sweet cream
1½ lbs. raisins
1 lbs. currants
½ cup citron
½ cup orange peel
½ tsp. nutmeg
Dash of salt

Cream the butter and sugar, add the beaten egg yolks, then alternately the cream and flour sifted with baking powder. Stir in the fruit, which has been dredged with flour, also the nutmeg, last of all the whites of eggs beaten to a stiff froth. Bake in deep pans lined with paraffin paper.

OLD FASHIONED GINGER CAKE OR BREAD

Cut up in a pan ½ cup of fresh butter, and ½ cup of brown sugar and beat to a cream with a paddle. Add one cup of homemade sorghum molasses, one heaping tsp. of cinnamon, mace and nutmeg, three tbsp. black coffee or one wine glass of brandy, beat three eggs until very light, and thick, three cups of flour, sifted and stirred alternately with the beaten eggs into the batter. Last, mix in the juice and grated rind of one orange. Dissolve one tsp. of soda in a little warm water and stir into the batter. Beat until very light. Bake in a loaf pan in a moderate oven. This was a party cake and was usually served with apple cider.

PORK CAKE, WITHOUT BUTTER, MILK, OR EGGS

"A most delightful cake is made by the use of pork, which saves the expense of butter, eggs and milk. It must be tasted to be appreciated; and another advantage if it is that you can make enough, some leisure day, to last the season through. Two months after being baked it has been found still nice and moist." (1900)

Fat, salt pork, entirely free of lean or rind, chopped so fine as to be almost like lard, 1 lb.; pour boiling water upon it, ½ pt.; raisins, seeded and chopped, 1 lb; citron, shaved into shreds, ¼ lb.; sugar, 2 cups; molasses, 1 cup; saleratus, 1 tsp., rubbed fine and put into the molasses. Mix these all together, and stir in sifted flour to make the consistency of common cake mixtures; then stir in nutmeg and cloves finely ground, 1 oz. each; cinnamon, also fine, 2 ozs.; be governed about the time of baking it by putting a sliver into it. When nothing adheres, it is done. It should be baked slowly.

You can substitute other fruit in place of the raisins, if desired, using as much or as little as you please, or none at all, and still have a nice cake. In this respect you may call it the accommodation cake, as it accommodates itself to the wishes or circumstances of its levers. When pork will do all we here claim for it, who will longer contend that it is not fit to eat? Who?

1900 BRIDE CAKE

"The bride came home, and took dinner with her family, one year from the marriage; and her mother set on some of the cake, as nice and moist as when baked."

Take butter, 1½ lbs; sugar, 1½ lbs., half of which is to be Orleans sugar; eggs, well beaten, 2 lbs.; raisins, 4 lbs., having the seeds taken out, and chopped; English currants having the grit picked out, and nicely washed, 5 lbs.; citron, cut fine, 2 lbs.; sifted flour, 2 lbs.; nutmegs, 2 in number, and mace, as much in bulk; alcohol, 1 gill to ½ pt., in which a dozen or 15 drops of oil of lemon have been put.

When ready to make your cake, weigh your butter and cut it in pieces, and put it where it will soften, but not melt. Next, stir the butter to a cream, and then add the sugar, and work till white. Next beat the yolks of the eggs, and put them to the sugar and butter. Meanwhile another person should beat the whites to a stiff froth, and put them in. Then add the spices and flour, and, last of all the fruit, except the citron, which is to be put in about three layers, the bottom layer about one inch from the bottom, and the top one an inch from the top, and the other in the middle, smoothing the top of the cake by dipping a spoon or two of water upon it for that purpose. The pan in which it is baked should be about thirteen inches across the top, and five and a half or six inches deep, without scallops, and two–three quart pans also, which it will fill; and they will require to be slowly baked about three or four hours. But it is impossible to give definite rules as to the time required in baking cake. Try whether the cake is done, by piercing it with a broom splinter, and if nothing adheres, it is done. Butter the cake pans well; or if the pans are lined with buttered white paper, the cake will be less liable to burn. Moving cakes while baking tends to make them heavy.

["The price of a large 'Bride Cake,' like this, would be about twelve dollars, and the cost of making it would be about three dollars only, with your two small ones, which would cost as much to buy them as it does to make the whole three."]

FROSTING WITHOUT EGGS

1 cup granulated sugar, dampened with 5 large tbsp. of milk; boil five minutes without stirring; set the dish in cold water; add flavoring and beat constantly until it becomes a thick creamy frosting.

CREAM FILLING FOR LAYER CAKE

1 pt. new milk; 2 eggs; 3 tbsp. sifted flour; 1 cup sugar. Stir all into a little of the cold milk; boiling the remainder; then cook all together to a thick custard; flavor when cool. If desired add hickory or other nut meats chopped fine.

ROSE COLORING FOR FROSTING, JELLIES, ICE CREAM, ETC.

¼ each cream Tartar and pow'd. alum; 1 oz. pow'd. cochineal; 4 oz. loaf sugar and a saltspoonful soda. Boil 10 minutes in a pint of soft water. Cool and bottle for use.

THREE EGG BAKE

Margaret Youngblood Stiles, ca. 1880

Whites of three eggs, two cups flour (scant), 1 cup of sweet milk, 1½ cups sugar, ½ cup of butter or ⅓ of lard, two level tsp. baking powder. Mix and bake at moderate temperature.

"FILLING"

¾ cups sugar, ¾ cups of milk, yolks of three eggs, tbsp. flour. Boil until thick. Then add one tsp. extract.

Cookies

OLD FASHION MOLASSES COOKIES
Used by five generations of the Halliburton-Elliot Family

8 cups all purpose flour
4 tsp. soda (level)
Pinch of salt
1 tbsp. ginger
1 tsp. cinnamon

3 cups sorgum molasses
1 cup lard melted
½ cup butter melted
10 tbsp. boiling water

Sift then measure the flour, sift again with soda, salt and spices. Combine molasses, melted lard, melted butter, and water. To this add 4 cups of the dry ingredients and blend well. Add remainder of flour mixture, blend well—let stand 1 hour in cool place. Turn out on floured board. Roll out, cut ¼-inch thick. Place on cooky tin. Sprinkle with sugar, cook in hot oven

SORGUM GINGER BREAD
Halliburton Family

1 cup sorgum molasses
1 cup sugar
1 cup buttermilk
1 cup butter or lard
3 eggs
1 tbsp. ginger

1 tbsp. soda
1 tsp. cinnamon
1 tsp. cloves
Pinch of salt
5 cups sifted flour

Mix all and bake in quick oven.

ORANGE COOKIES
Edith Miller Dixon

Cream ½ cup butter, 1 cup sugar, 1 egg, grated rind of 1 orange, ¼ tsp. soda in ½ cup thick sour cream. And add 1 tsp. orange juice, 2½ cups flour, ¼ tsp. salt, 3 tsp. baking powder. Sift, mix and beat till smoothe. Drop from teaspoon onto greased baking sheet, 1½ inch apart. Sprinkle sugar on top. Bake 12 minutes in moderate oven, makes 6 dozen cookies.

GREAT-GRANDMOTHER TENERY'S OATMEAL COOKIES
Navarro County, TX, 1880

1 cup butter	2 tbsp. cocoa
2 cups sugar	2 large eggs
1 tsp. cinnamon	1 cup raisins
1 tsp. soda	2 cups oatmeal
1 tsp. baking powder	2 cups flour
1 tbsp. vanilla	1 cup chopped pecans

Cream butter and sugar, add eggs, one at a time and beat thoroughly. Sift dry ingredients three times and add to creamed mixture with oatmeal, pecans and raisins. Drop on greased tins, and bake in moderate oven for 15 minutes.

PECAN MACAROONS
Marie Klein Streuer

1 lb. coarsely chopped pecans	4 egg whites
1 lb. powdered sugar	2 pieces dry toast, ground
¼ tsp. cinnamon	to make fine crumbs

Beat the egg whites until stiff (the consistency of thick whipped cream). Gradually add the sugar and cinnamon. Fold in bread crumbs, then pecans. Drop by rounded teaspoonfuls onto greased cookie sheets. Bake in slow oven for 15 to 25 minutes, depending on the size of the cookie. Remove from pan immediately, cool on rack. Makes 3 to 4 dozen depending on size. Store in a tightly sealed container.

[It was originally made with homemade cracked wheat bread.]

EDNA'S ICE BOX COOKIES

Tante Edna Nowotny Voigt

1 lb. brown sugar	½ tsp. soda mixed with
1 lb. butter	1 tbsp. hot water
1 egg, slightly beaten	2 cups chopped pecans
1 tsp. vanilla	6 cups all purpose flour

Cream butter and sugar, add egg, vanilla, soda and water; mix well, then work in flour, 1 cup at a time. Mix thoroughly. Mix in pecans and shape into rolls. Chill for 24 hours or more. Slice about ¼" thick and place on greased cookie sheet. Bake in moderate oven about 12 to 15 minutes. Cool cookies on pan for a few minutes then finish cooling on a rack. Store in a tightly sealed container.

["This is a special recipe that our dear Tante Edna made for all special occasions, and she usually had some ready when we stopped by to visit. She was always ready to share this recipe."]

PFEFFERNUSSE (PEPPERNUTS)

2¼ cups sifted flour	2 eggs
2 tsp. cinnamon	1 cup sugar
2 tsp. cloves	1 cup finely chopped pecans
½ tsp. mace	1 tsp. grated lemon rind
¼ tsp. black pepper	½ cup slivered citron

Sift flour, measure and sift together with remaining dry ingredients. Beat eggs till fluffy, add sugar and cream well. Add dry ingredients and pecans, lemon rind and citron. Combine and chill at least ½ hour (up to several hours). Cut with a floured small round cutter at least 1" thick. Place on cloth covered cookie sheets about 2" apart. Let stand for 24 hours. When

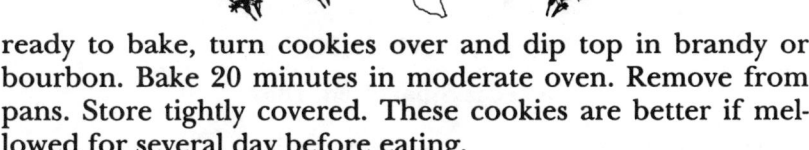

ready to bake, turn cookies over and dip top in brandy or bourbon. Bake 20 minutes in moderate oven. Remove from pans. Store tightly covered. These cookies are better if mellowed for several day before eating.

PECAN PRALINE COOKIES

1 cup brown sugar, packed
1 tbsp. flour
½ tsp. salt
1 egg white stiffly beaten
1 tsp. vanilla
3 cups pecans

Add vanilla to stiffly beaten egg white. Fold in sugar, salt, and add nuts dusted with flour. Place small clusters on greased baking sheets. Bake in slow oven for about 20-30 minutes. Remove from baking sheets and cool on rack. Pack in covered jar or tin. Delicious.

LEBKUCHEN

1 cup honey
¾ cup brown sugar
1 egg
1 tbsp. lemon juice
1 tsp. grated lemon rind
2¾ cups flour
½ tsp. soda
½ tsp. salt
1 tsp. baking powder
1 tsp. cinnamon
1 tsp. nutmeg
1 tsp. cloves
1 tsp. allspice
⅓ cup finely chopped citron
⅓ cup chopped pecans

Mix and add dry ingredients. Mix in citron and nuts. Chill overnight. Rollout a small amount at a time, keeping rest chilled. Roll 1¼" inch thick and cut in squares or fancy shapes. Place on greased cookie sheets. Bake in moderate oven for 10-12 minutes. Glaze with powdered sugar frosting. Decorate with candied fruit.

OATMEAL ROCKS
Rebecca Stuart Red, 1852

1 cup shortening
1 cup white sugar
1 cup brown sugar
4 eggs
4 cups flour
4 cups oatmeal

1 tsp. salt
1 tsp. soda
1 tsp. vanilla
2 cups nuts (pecans)
1 cup raisins

Cream shortening with white sugar, then brown sugar. Add eggs, flour, a little at a time with salt, soda and vanilla. Add oatmeal, a little at a time. Mix with hands. Add nuts and raisins. Drop on cookie sheet with spoon, or roll into ball with hands. Cook in moderate oven for 15 minutes or until done. Makes about 48 cookies.

["Used on the farm at Gay Hill by Rebecca Stuart Red who came to Texas in 1852 with a diploma and started teaching college-level courses. Since her mother died when she was 8 years old, she became a really good cook."]

CINNAMON STARS

6 egg whites
1 lb. powdered sugar, sifted
Grated rind of 1 lemon

1½ lbs. finely ground pecans
or almonds

Beat egg whites until frothy. Gradually add the powdered sugar, starting with a tbsp. at a time. Beat until mixture is stiff and glossy. Add the cinnamon and lemon rind and continue beating about 15 minutes. Put aside one-third of the mixture to use for the topping or frosting. Fold pecans or almonds in the remaining egg white mixture. Pat a little dough in the palm of your floured hand and shape into star. (*Note:* the dough should be patted about ¼" to ½" thick. This method makes the cookie lighter and more chewy than rolling out on a floured board.) Place on a greased cookie sheet.

Frost cookies with reserved egg white mixture. Start spreading from the center and work out to the points. Bake in moderate oven for 15 to 25 minutes depending on the thickness — or until beige and topping looks crusty. We bake a test cookie first. Cool on rack. Handle cookies with care, they are very fragile. Store in a sealed container. Makes about 36 large stars.

["This cookie recipe was brought from Hattenheim, Nassau, Germany, by our great, great grandmother in 1845. She was one of the original 200 that founded New Braunfels. This cookie is the most time consuming of all the dozens of varieties of cookies that were made by our grandmothers and descendants. They were always made for special days, such as birthdays and anniversaries, in heart shapes. Each large star cookie is as generous as a piece of pie or cake and the tradition continues still."]

ROUGH AND READY CAKE

Butter or lard, 1 lb.; molasses, 1 qt.; soda, 1 oz.; milk or water, ½ pt.; ground ginger, 1 tbsp.; and a little oil of lemon; flour sufficient.

Mix up the ginger in flour, and rub the butter or lard in, also dissolve the soda in the milk or water; put in the molasses, and use the flour in which the ginger and butter is rubbed up, and sufficient more to make the dough of a proper consistence to roll out; cut the cakes out with a long narrow cutter, and wet the top with a little molasses and water, to remove the flour from the cake; turn the top down into pulverized white sugar, and place in an oven sufficiently hot for bread, but keep them in only to bake, not to dry up.

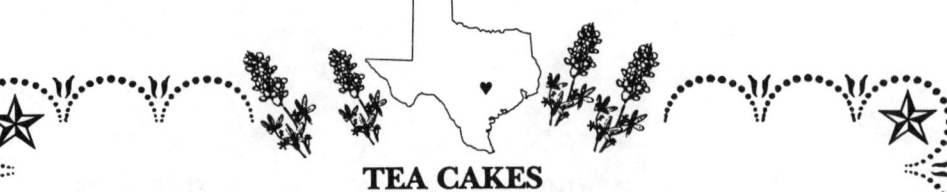

TEA CAKES

This recipe belonged to Helen Murchison. She always had a flour sack filled with these delicious treats hanging behind the kitchen door.

1 scant cup butter
1 scant cup sugar
2½ cups flour
1 beaten egg

Pinch of salt
2 tsp. baking powder
Vanilla or lemon extract

Cream butter, sugar and eggs. Sift flour, baking powder and salt together—add this mixture alternately with milk to butter, sugar and egg. Beat together and add extra flour if needed to roll out dough. Roll and cut out cakes. Bake in moderate oven until lightly brown.

BERRY TEA CAKES
1900

1 cup sugar
1½ cups milk
Piece of butter size of an eggs

2 eggs
1 heaping tsp. baking powder
Flour to make stiff batter

Into this stir a pint of fresh berries, without the juice, bake like muffins. Eat warm with butter.

Puddings

☆ ☆ ☆

SAVING

"Saving is a more difficult art than earning, some people put dimes into their pies and puddings, where other put in cents; the cent dishes are the most healthy."

☆ ☆ ☆

RICE BLANC MANGE

Sarah Stafford Dyer and Jeanette Dyer Davis, 1849

Sarah Stafford Dyer and family came to Texas with Stephen F. Austin's Colonists.

Boil a teacup full of rice in a very small quantity of water till it is near bursting—then add half a pint of milk, boil it to a mush. Stirring all the time; season it with sugar, wine, and nutmeg, dip the mold in water, and fill it; when cold, turn it in a dish and surround it with boiled custard seasoned—or syllabub—garnish it with marmalade.

SWEET POTATO PUDDING

Grandmother Burleson's recipe

1½ sugar
½ cup molasses
⅓ cup butter, melted
1 tsp. nutmeg
1 tsp. cinnamon

Good pinch salt
3 eggs, beaten
1½ cups milk
4 cups grated raw sweet potatoes

Combine: sugar, molasses, butter, spices and salt. Add eggs and milk. Stir in yams (potatoes) mixing thoroughly. Pour into (greased) bowl. Bake in moderate oven for 1½ hours. Serve warm or cold with heavy cow cream. 6 servings. This was a favorite during Christmas holidays.

WOODFORD PUDDING

3 eggs
1 cup sugar
1 tsp. soda, dissolved in
   3 tsps. sour milk
½ cup butter
1 cup flour

1 cup jam or preserves
(green mustang grape
preserves are delicious
in the pudding)
Spices & nutmeg to taste
(cinnamon, cloves, allspice)

Mix well—bake slowly in pudding pan. Sauce: 2 egg whites (unbeaten), stir in gradually 1 cup sugar. Beat till light and puffy. When ready to serve, add vanilla to taste and ¾ cup rich cream.

DATE PUDDING

ca. 1885

Three-fourths cup sugar; four well beaten eggs; one pint chopped nuts; one pint chopped dates; three tbsp. flour on dates; vanilla flavoring.

Bake carefully in well greased pan.

APPLE FLOAT
Mrs. J. W. Smith, 1891

Take a quart of stewed apples, press them through a sieve, sweeten and flavor to taste; then beat into them the well-frothed whites of three or four eggs. Beat well, and pile in a glass bowl half filled with cream or rich milk.

EDNA ROGERS ALEXANDER'S BREAD PUDDING

3 eggs
1 tsp. vanilla
¾ cup sugar

¾ cup raisins
Bread
Milk

Bake in moderate oven for 1 hour. Sauce: 1 cup sugar, 2 tbsp. cornstarch, 2 tbsp. butter, 2 cups water; bring to a boil and cook until thick. Pour over bread pudding. Granny always made this at family get togethers.

TAPIOCA PUDDING
Mrs. John Webb

One cup of tapioca, the coarse kind is preferable, soaked all night in sufficient water to cover it. Then add one quart of preserved strawberries, or any kind of good canned or stewed fruit, cut fine if pears or peaches, sweeten to taste. Cook 1½ hours in a moderate oven. Meringue improves it. Serve with whipped or plain cream. This is wholesome and very nice.

ITALIAN SNOW
Mrs. Paul Thornton, 1891

Soak one-half box of "Cox's Gelatine" in a pint of cold water until thoroughly dissolved, then add whites of three eggs well beaten, one cup of sugar, flavoring of any kind of extract; beat with egg beater for twenty (20) minutes. Pour into molds to cool. To be eaten with cream.

FLOATING ISLAND

3 eggs, 6 tbsp. sugar, pinch of salt, 2 cups milk, vanilla, a little jelly. Beat the egg yokes slightly, add sugar and salt; add 2 cups scalded milk. Cook in double boiler until it thickens and forms a coating on spoon. Pour at once into shallow baking dish. Beat egg whites, add 6 tbsp. sugar, vanilla, place spoonfuls on custard, dab jelly on each island. Brown for 12 or 15 minutes.

ORIOLES NEST
Mrs. L. S. Ross, 1891

Mold blanc mange in egg shells, having emptied and washed as many of them as will make a pretty nest. Having made a stiff jelly, partly fill a bowl with it and place the egg shapes upon it, in such a way as to look well when turned out. All around and over the eggs place long strips of preserved orange rind to resemble straw. Melt a cupful of the jelly reserved for the purpose and pour over the whole. After it is thoroughly congealed, turn out upon a glass dish.

BREADED TOMATO PUDDING
Lel Red Purcell (1859–1946)

Use real ripe tomatoes (any amount desired), 4 or 5 slices of old bread to absorb the juice, ½ to 1 cup sugar (sweeten to taste).

Bring to boil on stove and cook 3–5 minutes.

["When tomatoes were grown on the farm at Lockhart, Lel Red Purcell used ripe tomatoes split by weather."]

ENGLISH PLUM PUDDING
Margaret Youngblood Stiles, ca. 1885

Two cups of bread crumbs, one cup of chop suet, one cup of molasses, one cup sweet milk, one cup each currents and raisins or citron and nuts, one heaping tsp. baking powder, one tsp. cinnamon or allspice, three eggs and flour enough to make a good batter. Steam three or four hours.

SAUCE FOR PLUM PUDDING

Yolks of four eggs well beaten, one cup sugar, one cup sweet milk, and ½ cup butter.
   Cook until thick as cream, add whiskey or brandy.

BAKED CORN MEAL PUDDING
A very early family recipe.

Take a large cupful of yellow meal and a teacupful of cooking molasses and beat them well together; then add to them a quart of boiling milk, some salt and a large tbsp. of powdered ginger, add a cupful of finely-chopped suet or a piece of butter the size of an egg. Butter a brown earthen pan and turn the pudding in, let it stand until it thickens; then as you put it into the oven, turn over it a pint of cold milk, but do not stir it, as this makes the jelly. Bake three hours. Serve warm with hard sauce.

DELICATE INDIAN PUDDING
1899

One quart milk, two heaping tbsp. of Indian meal, four of sugar, one of butter, three eggs, one tsp. of salt. Boil milk in double boiler, sprinkle the meal into it, stirring often. Beat together the eggs, salt, sugar and ½ tsp. of ginger. Stir the butter into the meal and milk. Pour this gradually over the egg mixture. Bake slowly one hour. Serve with sauce of heated syrup and butter.

COTTAGE PUDDING

One heaping pint of flour, half a cupful of sugar, one cupful of milk, one tsp. of soda dissolved in the milk, one tbsp. of butter, two tsp. of cream of tartar rubbed dry in the flour; flavor with nutmeg; bake in a moderate oven; cut in slices and serve warm with wine or brandy sauce, or sweet sugar sauce.

ROSE BRANDY

Gather the leaves of roses while the dew is on them, and as soon as they open put them into a wide-mouthed bottle, and when the bottle is full pour in the best of fourth proof French brandy. It will be fit for use in three or four weeks and may be frequently replenished. It is sometimes considered preferable to wine as a flavoring to pastries and pudding sauces (for cakes and puddings).

Pastry, Pies, and Tarts

☆ ☆ ☆

THE ART OF COOKING

"The great aim of all cooking is to retain all the valuable elements of the food and to put them into such forms as shall awake desire, stimulate digestion, and secure to the eater, in the readiest and most pleasing way, all the nutriment these viands afford."

☆ ☆ ☆

DEEP FRIED APPLE PIES

3 cups sliced, peeled tart apples
½ cup water
1 tsp. lemon juice (freshly squeezed)
¼ cup sugar
½ tsp. cinnamon
⅛ tsp. nutmeg
Pastry for double crust
Shortening
Butter
Powdered sugar

Put apples into a saucepan; add water and lemon juice. Cover tightly and cook over low heat until tender (about 15 minutes). Drain the apples and add sugar, cinnamon and nutmeg. Divide pastry into two balls. Flatten one ball at a time on a lightly floured surface and roll out ⅛-inch thick. Cut out rounds, using a 3½-inch cutter. Heat shortening to moderate heat. Place 2 tbsp. apple mixture on each pastry round; dot with butter, moisten half of the edge of each round with water. Fold the other half over the fruit. Press edges together with a fork to seal tightly. Lower the pies into hot lard. Fry about 3 minutes or until golden brown. Turn the pies as they rise to the top. Do not pierce the crust. Remove pies and drain on absorbent paper. Sprinkle with powdered sugar. Serve warm.

GREEN GRAPE PIE

When the mustang grapes on the creek reached the size of a small green pea, we gathered a bucketful, and mother would make us a wonderful treat - green grape pie.

Three pints green mustang grapes washed and stemmed, 2½ cups sugar, ½ cup butter, 2 tbsp. flour or cornstarch, juice from half lemon and recipe for 2 pie crust. Put grapes in sauce pan and add water to almost cover. Add sugar and heat until sugar melts. Dissolve flour in small amount of water—beat till smooth and stir into grape mixture and cook a few minutes. Add lemon juice and pour into baking pan or casserole, drop bits of pastry into grape mixture—cover cobbler with remaining pastry, brush with butter and sprinkle with sugar. Bake in moderately hot oven until pastry is brown.

SWEET POTATO PIE

1½ cup cooked sweet potatoes
¾ cup sugar
Pinch of salt
1 tsp. cinnamon
3 eggs
2 tbsp. butter

Mash sweet potatoes until free of lumps, add sugar, salt, cinnamon and beaten eggs, add milk and butter. Mix well, pour into pastry lined pie pan. Bake in medium hot oven until knife blade comes out clean.

PUMPKIN PIE

*"What moistens the lips, and brightens the eye
What calls back the past like the rich pumpkin pie?"*

Three cups of stewed pumpkin, two cups of boiled milk, three eggs, one cup sugar, ½ cup sorghum molasses, butter the size of a walnut, ½ tsp. cinnamon. Mix all together, place in a pie crust and bake. This is sufficient for three pies. To make extra nice, after pie is baked remove from the oven and cover top with ground pecans and replace in the oven and bake for a short time until the pecans are just slightly browned.

PEARL DONNA'S PECAN PIE

Mix: 2 tbsp. sugar, 2 tbsp. flour, 1 tsp. flour, 1 tsp. nutmeg, beat 2 eggs and add to mixture. Add 1 cup white syrup, 1 tbsp. melted butter, 1 tsp. vanilla; mix, and add 1 cup chopped pecans. Bake in moderate oven for about 40 minutes. Use unbaked pie shell.

TEXAS BUTTERMILK PIE

1 cup sugar	1 cup buttermilk
4 tbsp. flour	1 teaspoon vanilla
½ cup melted butter	Dash of nutmeg
3 eggs beaten	9-inch uncooked pie shell

Preheat oven, mix sugar and flour, add cooled butter, beaten eggs, buttermilk and vanilla. Mix and pour into pie shell. Bake 15 minutes in moderate oven. Turn oven down to moderately slow oven and bake 25 minutes. Cool. Slice when cool.

OLD, OLD PIE CRUST RECIPE
Very good For Fryed Pies, 1850

5 cups flour	1 tbsp. sugar
1 cup lard	1 pint of milk
1 tbsp. baking powder	2 eggs well beaten
1 tbsp. salt	

Mix milk and eggs to dry ingredients — mix well — roll out. Cut six-inch round circles, fill half full of fruit or cream pie filling, fold over and crimp edges, prick with fork, fry in boiling grease — dip out and place on towel when golden brown.

["These are very good for lunch boxes – from my old collection" – Alline Halliburton Elliot]

GREEN GRAPE COBBLER
Recipe used by Nancy Kincheloe Green in Llano County, 1840s

3 cups green wild Mustang grapes, picked and washed.	2 cups sugar
¼ to ½ cup flour	Water
Butter	Pastry for 2 crust pie using lard.

Grapes must be picked before seeds become firm — late May or early June in Central Texas. Cook grapes, sugar and small amount of water for 5 to 7 minutes. Mix flour with ¼ cup water and add to mixture. Add additional water if needed for juice. Taste test for sweetness desired. Layer strips of pastry alternately with grape mixture, ending with pastry. Dot with butter. Bake in a medium hot oven until brown. Approximately 30 to 40 minutes.

APPLE CUSTARD PIE
1900

Three cupfuls of milk, four eggs and one cupful of sugar, two cupfuls of thick stewed apples, strained through a colander. Beat the whites and yolks of the eggs lightly and mix the yolks well with the apples, flavoring with nutmeg. Then beat into this the milk, and lastly, the whites. Let the crust partly bake before turning in this filling. To be baked with only the one crust, like all custard pies.

APPLE AND PEACH MERINGUE PIE

Stew the apples or peaches and sweeten to taste. Mash smooth and season with nutmeg. Fill the crusts and bake until just done. Put on no top crust. Take the whites of three eggs for each pie and whip to a stiff froth, and sweeten with three tbsp. of powdered sugar. Flavor with rose-water or vanilla; beat until it will stand alone; then spread it on the pie one-half to one inch thick; set it back into the oven until the meringue is well "set." Eat cold.

LEMON CUSTARD PIE
Octavia Moore Proctor, 1891

Two cups of sugar, five eggs, one heaping tbsp. of butter, the rind and juice of two lemons. Beat well the yolks, sugar and butter together, add the whites beaten to a stiff froth, then add the rind and juice of the two lemons. Use rich pastry.

LEMON PIE
1897

Take a deep dish, grate into it the outside of the rind of two lemons; add to that a cup and a half of white sugar, two heaping tbsp. of unsifted flour, or one of cornstarch; stir it well together, then add the yolks of three well-beaten eggs, beat this thoroughly, then add the juice of the lemons, two cups of water and a piece of butter the size of a walnut. Set this on the fire in another dish containing boiling water and cook it until it thickens, and will dip up on the spoon like cold honey. Remove it from the fire, and cooled, pour it into a deep pie-tin, lined with pastry; bake, and when done, have ready the whites, beaten stiff, with three small tbsp. of sugar. Spread this over the top and return to the oven to set and brown slightly. This makes a deep, large sized pie, and very superior.

MRS. CONLEY'S LEMON PIE

Make large crust and bake.

Filling:

6 egg yolks — well beaten
1 cup sugar
1 lemon rind and juice of two lemons
2 tbsp. of water

Cook the above in double boiler until thick as mush.

6 egg whites
1 cup sugar

While above cooked mixture is hot, beat in ½ of the meringue and put in crust. Cook in slow oven twenty minutes. Add top meringue and brown.

JELLY PIES

Mrs. C. R. Gibson, 1891

One cup jelly, one cup sugar, ½ cup butter, five eggs. Line pie plates with rich crust. Pour half in each of two plates, and bake slowly.

MARGARET YOUNGBLOOD STILES' PECAN PIE
ca. 1885

One pint sweet milk; yolks of three eggs; ¾ cup sugar; two tbsp. flour; 1½ cups pecans. Let boil and pour in cooked pie crust. Make a meringue of the whites of eggs and pour over pies when cooked. Let brown in piping oven.

CUSTARD PIE

Beat together until very light the yolks of four eggs and four tbsp. of sugar, flavor with nutmeg or vanilla; then add the four beaten whites, a pinch of salt and, lastly, a quart of sweet milk; mix well and pour into tins lined with paste. Bake until firm.

BOSTON CREAM PIE
1897

Cream Part: Put on a pint of milk to boil. Break two eggs into a dish and add one cup of sugar and ½ cup of flour previously mixed after beating well, stir it into the milk just as the milk commences to boil; add an ounce of butter and keep on stirring one way until it thickens; flavor with vanilla or lemon.

Crust Part: Three eggs beaten separately, one cup of granulated sugar, 1½ cups of sifted flour, one large tsp. of baking powder and two tbsp. of milk or water. Divide the batter in half and bake on two medium-sized pie-tins. Bake in a rather quick oven to a straw color. When done and cool, split each one in half with a sharp broad-bladed knife, and spread half the cream between each. Serve cold.

GREEN TOMATO PIE

Take medium-sized tomatoes, pare and cut out the stem end. Having your pie-pan lined with paste made as biscuit dough, slice the tomatoes very thin, filling the pan somewhat heaping, then grate over it a nutmeg; put in half a cup of butter and a medium cup of sugar, if the pan is rather deep. Sprinkle a small handful of flour over all, pouring in half a cup of vinegar before adding the top crust. Bake half an hour in a moderately hot oven, serving hot.

[Is good; try it.]

GRAPE PIE
1899

Pop the pulps out of the skins into one dish and put the skins into another. Then simmer the pulp a little over the fire to soften it; remove it and rub it through a colander to separate it from the seeds. Then put the skins and pulp together and they are ready for pies or for canning or putting in jugs for other use. Fine for pies.

MINCE MEAT FOR PIES
Mrs. C. R. Gibson, 1891

Three lbs. beef tongue, well minced; three lbs. suet, well minced; six lbs. stewed apples, three lbs. preserved peaches, two lbs. winter grapes, six lbs. brown sugar, two nutmegs, six tbsp. of cinnamon, six dozen cloves, four tbsp. of spice, four tbsp. of mace, one qt. of vinegar, three pints of whisky, half lb. citron, three oranges, six green apples, two lbs. stoned raisins, two lbs. currants.

RIPE BERRY PIE

All made the same as "Cherry Pie." Line your pie-tin with crust, fill half full of berries, shake over a tbsp. of sifted flour (if very juicy) and as much sugar as is necessary to sweeten sufficiently. Now fill up the crust to the top, making quite full. Cover with crust and bake about forty minutes.

Huckleberry and blackberry pies are improved by putting into them a little ginger and cinnamon.

PEACH PIE
ca. 1900

Peel, stone and slice the peaches. Line a pie plate with crust and lay in your fruit, sprinkling sugar liberally over them in proportion to their sweetness. Allow three peach kernels chopped fine to each pie; pour in a very little water and bake with an upper crust, or with cross-bars of paste across the top.

STEWED PUMPKIN OR SQUASH FOR PIES

Deep colored pumpkins are generally the best. Cut a pumpkin or squash in half, take out the seeds, then cut it up in thick slices, pare the outside and cut again in small pieces. Put it into a large pan or saucepan with a very little water; let it cook slowly until tender. Now set the pot on the back of the stove, where it will not burn, and cook slowly, stirring often until the moisture is dried out and the pumpkin looks dark and red. It requires cooking a long time, at least half a day, to have it dry and rich. When cool press through a colander.

PUMPKIN PIE
1900

One quart of stewed pumpkin pressed through a sieve, nine eggs, whites and yolks beaten separately, two scant quarts of milk, one tsp. of mace, one tsp. of cinnamon and the same of nutmeg, 1½ cups of white sugar, or very light brown. Beat all well together and bake in crust without cover.

A tbsp. of brandy is a great improvement to pumpkin or squash pies.

OSGOOD PIES

2 cups sugar
½ cup butter
4 eggs
1 cup nuts
1 cup raisins
1 tsp. cinnamon
½ tsp. cloves

Cream sugar and butter, add spices, well beaten yolks, raisins and nuts. Then add stiffly beaten whites. If it is too thick, thin with a little water. This recipe makes 2 pies.

MRS. TEN EVCK'S MOLASSES PIE
1891

One cup of sugar, one cup of molasses, one tbsp. melted butter, four eggs; beat yolks and sugar very light; add the molasses, butter, and flavor with vanilla; beat the whites to a stiff froth, and stir in thoroughly and bake in one crust. This makes one pie.

FINE PUFF PASTRY

This recipe I purchased from a cook on one of the Lake Michigan steamers many years ago, and it is, without exception, the finest puff paste I have ever seen.

Into one quart of sifted flour mix two tsp. of baking powder and a tsp. of salt; then sift again. Measure out one teacupful of butter and one of lard, hard and cold. Take the lard and rub into the flour until a very fine smooth paste. Then put in just enough ice-water, say half a cupful, containing a beaten white of egg, to mix a very stiff dough. Roll it out into a thin sheet, spread with one-fourth of the butter, sprinkle over with a little flour, then roll up closely in a long roll, like a scroll, double the ends towards the centre, flatten and re-roll. Then spread again with another quarter of the butter. Repeat this operation until the butter is used up. Put it on an earthen dish, cover it with a cloth and set it in a cold place; let it remain until cold; an hour or more before making out the crust. Tarts made with this paste cannot be cut with a knife when fresh; they go into flakes at the touch. You may roll this pastry in any direction, from you, toward you, sideways, any way, it matters not, but you must have nice flour, ice-water and very little of it, and strength to roll it, if you would succeed.

RULES FOR UNDER CRUST

A good rule for pie crust for a pie requiring only an under crust, as a custard or pumpkin pie, is: Three large tbsp. of flour, sifted, rubbing into it a large tbsp. of cold butter, or part butter and part lard, and a pinch of salt, mixing with cold water enough to form a smooth, stiff paste, and rolled quite thin.

STRAWBERRY TARTLETS

Tarts of strawberry or any other kind of preserves are generally made of the trimmings of puff paste rolled a little thicker than the ordinary pies; then cut out with a round cutter, first dipped in hot water, to make the edges smooth, and placed in small tart-pans, first pricking a few holes at the bottom with a fork before placing them in the oven. Bake from ten to fifteen minutes. Let the paste cool a little; then fill it with preserve. By this manner, both the flavor and color of the jam are preserved, which would be lost were it baked in the oven on the paste; and, besides, so much jam is not required.

TARTS

ca. 1898

Larger pans are required for tarts proper, the size of small, shallow pie-tins; then after the paste is baked and cooled and filled with the jam or preserve, a few stars or leaves are placed on the top, or strips of paste, criss-crossed on the top, all of which have been previously baked on a tin by themselves.

FRUIT TURNOVERS

Make a nice puff paste; roll it out the usual thickness, as for pies; then cut it out into circular pieces about the size of a small tea saucer; pile the fruit on half of the paste, sprinkle over some sugar, wet the edges and turn the paste over. Press the edges together, ornament them and brush the turnovers over with the white of an egg; sprinkle over sifted sugar and bake on tins, in a brisk oven, for about twenty minutes. Instead of putting the fruit in raw, it may be boiled down with a little sugar first and then enclosed in the crust; or jam of any kind may be substituted for fresh fruit. These are suitable for taking on picnics.

ORANGE TARTLETS

Take the juice of two large oranges and the grated peel of one, ¾ of a cup of sugar, a tbsp. of butter; stir in a good tsp. of cornstarch into the juice of half a lemon and add to the mixture. Beat all well together and bake in tart shells. without cover.

MAIDS OF HONOR
1899

Take one cupful of sour milk, one of sweet milk, a tbsp. of melted butter, the yolks of four eggs, juice and rind of one lemon and a small cupful of white pounded sugar. Put both kinds of milk together in a vessel, which is set in another and let it become sufficiently heated to set the curd, then strain off the milk, rub the curd through a strainer, add butter to the curd, the sugar, well beaten eggs and lemon. Line the little pans with the richest of puff paste and fill with the mixture; bake until firm in the centre, from ten to fifteen minutes.

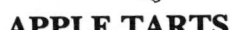

APPLE TARTS

Pare, quarter, core and boil in half a cupful of water, until quite soft, ten large, tart apples; beat until very smooth and add the yolks of six eggs, or three whole ones, the juice and grated outside rind of two lemons, half a cup of butter, 1½ cups of sugar (or more, if not sufficiently sweet); beat all thoroughly, line patty-pans with a puff paste and fill; bake five minutes in a hot oven.

Meringue: If desired very nice, cover them when removed from the oven with the meringue made of the whites of three eggs remaining, mixed with three tbsp. of sugar; return to the oven and delicately brown.

BLACKBERRY COBBLER

Our Grandmother Lee had her own blackberry patch by the cement tank where we all went swimming; our grandmother swam in the tank every morning even if she had to break the ice.

4 cups of fresh blackberries
¾ cup sugar to 1 cup depending upon how sour the fruit.

Simmer blackberries and sugar plus 1 cup water until starting to boil. Heat oven to moderate temperature, butter 9 x 13-inch baking dish or pan, pour in fruit to cover. Make pie pastry and cut into 1½-inch strips, lay over fruit and brown in oven. Dip the rest of the fruit over browned strips, dot with butter. Add another layer of pastry strips, sprinkle with sugar and brown. Serve warm with whipped cream.

Custards, Creams, and Desserts for Levees and Other Occasions

A LEVEE AT THE PRESIDENT OF THE REPUBLIC OF TEXAS' HOUSE

[by Julia Lee Sinks who attended the levee as a young lady and later wrote articles about "Early Days in Texas" that were published in the *Galveston News*, 1896.]

President Lamar held a levee in the President's house. It was a beautiful night on the 15th of August, 1841. The pathway up the hillside was thronged until the parlors were filled to over flowing. The young people flitted in and out and stood in merry groups around the hilltop, lapped in the soft, satiny folds of Texas moonlight whose whiteness seemed almost palpable to the touch. What the infant republic lacked in house-room – nature supplied. And to such fullness, with her breeze of balm and the downy softness of her moonbeams that no need of lordly halls was felt. In one of the postoaks in the yard two mocking birds were rivaling each other in melody, perhaps incited by the music of the dancers within and the music of merry voices without. In the distance along the Colorado bottom the "Chick Will's Widow" sent up its mournful refrain to mingle with the other sounds of night, harmoniously answering the bursts of glee that bubbled and sparkled as if coming from the fountain of eternal youth. Here, perhaps, some one was singing one of the popular songs of the times; there, another group of two were talking in low confidential tones not unlike the tale of love. Perhaps it was – who knows?"

SOFT CARAMEL CUSTARD
1899

One quart of milk, half a cupful of sugar, six eggs, half a tsp. of salt. Put the milk on to boil, reserving a cupful. Beat the eggs and add the cold milk to them. Stir the sugar in a small frying pan until it becomes liquid and just begins to smoke. Stir it into the boiling milk; then add the beaten eggs and cold milk and stir constantly until the mixture begins to thicken. Set away to cool. Serve in glasses.

CUP CUSTARD

Six eggs, half a cupful of sugar, one quart of new milk. Beat the eggs and the sugar and milk, and any extract or flavoring you like. Fill your custard cups, sift a little nutmeg or cinnamon over the tops, set then in a moderate oven in a shallow pan half filled with hot water. In about twenty minutes try them with the handle of a teaspoon to see if they are firm. Judgment and great care are needed to attain skill in baking custard, for if left in the oven a minute too long, or if the fire is too hot, the milk will certainly whey.

Serve cold with fresh fruit sugared and placed on top of each. Strawberries, peaches or raspberries, as preferred.

APPLE CUSTARD

Pare, core and quarter a dozen large juicy pippins. Stew among them the yellow peel of a large lemon grated very fine, and stew them till tender in a very small portion of water. When done, mash them smooth with the back of a spoon (you must have a pint and half of the stewed apple); mix a half cupful of sugar with them and set them away till cold. Beat six eggs very light and stir them gradually into a quart of rich milk alternately with the stewed apple. Put the mixture into cups, or into a deep dish and bake it about twenty minutes. Send it to table cold, with nutmeg grated over the top.

CHARLOTTE RUSSE

Mrs. Rainey, 1891

Whip three pints of cream; sweeten and flavor to taste, the whites of six eggs well beaten, whip the cream and skim alternately, and mix well; dissolve one-half box of gelatine and stir rapidly.

WHIPPED CREAM

To the whites of three eggs, beaten to a stiff froth, add a pint of thick sweet cream (previously set where it is very cold) and four tbsp. of sweet wine, with three of fine white sugar and a tsp. of the extract of lemon or vanilla. Mix all the ingredients together on a board platter or pan and whip it to a standing froth; as the froth rises, take it off lightly with a spoon and lay it on an inverted sieve with a dish under it to catch what will drain through; and what drains through can be beaten over again.

Serve in a glass dish with jelly or jam and sliced sponge cake. This should be whipped in a cool place and set in the ice box.

BAVARIAN CREAM

One quart of sweet cream, the yolks of four eggs beaten together with a cupful of sugar. Dissolve half an ounce of gelatine or isinglass in half a teacupful of warm water; when it is dissolved stir in a pint of boiling hot cream; add the beaten yolks and sugar; cook all together until it begins to thicken, then remove from the fire and add the other pint of cold cream whipped to a stiff froth, adding a little at a time and beating hard. Season with vanilla or lemon. Whip the whites of the eggs for the top. Dip the mold in cold water before filling; set it in a cold place. To this could be added almonds, pounded, grated chocolate, peaches, pineapples, strawberries, raspberries, or any other seasonable fruit.

GELATINE JELLY WITHOUT BOILING
Mrs. Leslie Waggoner, 1891

To one box Cox's sparkling gelatine add one pint cold water; let it stand until dissolved, then add four pints boiling water, three lemons, juice and rind, two lbs. sugar; and one pint madeira wine. Stir well and strain.

PEACH CREAM

A quart of fine peaches, pare and stone the fruit and cut in quarters. Beat the whites of three eggs with a half cupful of powdered sugar until it is stiff enough to cut with a knife. Take the yolks and mix with half a cupful of granulated sugar and a pint of milk. Put the peaches into the mixture, place in a pudding-dish and bake until almost firm; then put in the whites, mixing all thoroughly again, and bake a light brown. Eat ice cold.

ORANGE TRIFLE

Take the parings from the outside of a dozen oranges and put to steep in a wide-mouthed bottle; cover it with good cognac and let it stand twenty-four hours; skin and seed the oranges and reduce to a pulp; press this through a sieve, sugar to taste, arrange in a dish and heap with whipped cream flavored with the orange brandy, place in a very cold place two hours before serving.

FRUIT TRIFLE

Whites of four eggs beaten to a stiff froth, two tbsp. each of sugar, currant jelly and raspberry jam. Eaten with sponge cakes, it is a delicious dessert.

MOONSHINE
Mrs. John Orr, 1891

This dessert combines a pretty appearance with a palatable flavor, and is a convenient substitute for ice cream. Beat whites of six eggs in large dish to a very stiff froth, add gradually six tbsp. of powdered sugar, beating for some time; then beat in half cup of jelly — acid preferred, such as grape or plum, set on ice until thoroughly chilled. In serving pour in each saucer some rich cream sweetened and flavored with vanilla, and in this cream pour a liberal portion of the moonshine. A rich boiled custard will answer in place of sweetened cream.

SPONGE CAKE

Separate the whites and yolks of six eggs. Beat the yolks to a cream, to which add two teacupfuls of powdered sugar, beating again from five to ten minutes, then add two tbsp. of milk or water, a pinch of salt and flavoring. Now add part of the beaten whites; then two cups of flour in which you have sifted two tsp. of baking powder; mix gradually into the above ingredients, stirring slowly and lightly, only enough to mix them well; lastly add the remainder of the whites of the eggs. Line the tins with buttered paper and fill two-thirds full.

CAKE AND SAUCE FOR DINNER
Mrs. I. V. Davis, 1891

Beat four eggs with 1½ cups of sugar; cream and add one cup butter and beat well together; mix with 2½ cups flour, in which has been sifted two tsp. yeast powder, and add half cup water. Warm and grease pan and bake in a gradually heating stove. *Sauce:* One cup sweet milk heated to near a boil, add 1½ cups sugar, and mace to flavor, and tbsp. butter.

LAURA DRISKILL'S MOONSHINE
1891

Beat the whites of six eggs in a large dish to a stiff froth, then add gradually six tbsp. powdered sugar (to make it thicker use more sugar), beat for thirty minutes, and then beat in one cup of jelly and set on ice until thoroughly chilled. In serving, pour in each saucer some whipped cream, flavored with lemon and vanilla, and on this place a liberal portion of the moonshine.

FLOATING ISLAND

One quart of milk, five eggs and five tbsp. of sugar. Scald the milk, then add the beaten yolks and one of the whites together with the sugar. First stir into them a little of the scalded milk to prevent curdling, then all of the milk. Cook it the proper thickness; remove from the fire, and when cool, flavor; then pour it into a glass dish and let it become very cold. Before it is served beat up the remaining whites of the eggs to a stiff froth and beat into them three tbsp. of sugar and two tbsp. of currant jelly, dip this over the top of the custard.

FRUIT BLANC MANGE

Stew nice, fresh fruit (cherries, raspberries and strawberries being the best); strain off the juice and sweeten to taste; place it over the fire in a double kettle until it boils; while boiling, stir in cornstarch wet with a little cold water, allowing two tbsp. of cornstarch to each pint of juice; continue stirring until sufficiently cooked; then pour into molds wet in cold water and set away to cool. Served with cream and sugar.

SPANISH CREAM
Mrs. Proctor, 1891

One half box of gelatine, soak in one-half pint of milk, then put one quart of milk on to boil, beat the whites of six eggs to a stiff froth; when the milk is boiling hot stir in the beaten yolks and sugar to taste, and the gelatine; let it thicken as you would soft custard, then pour it boiling hot on the whites, stirring all the time; flavor with vanilla, and pour into molds to cool. Let it stand at least twelve hours in a cold place before using.

HUEVOS REALES (ROYAL EGGS)
Mrs. Dr. Iglehart, 1891

Beat a dozen eggs until very light, then put them in a vessel, and again put this vessel in another of boiling water, to remain until well done. Put one-half pound of sugar into a pint of water to cook, until it makes a syrup; before it reaches the candied state, cut the yolks into shapes or small pieces, and put them into the syrup to boil. When cooked to a rich consistency, place on a dish, and on each piece of egg place blanched almonds and a few raisins.

COPAS MEXICANAS
Mrs. Dr. Iglehart, 1891

The yolks of twelve eggs beaten light, half pound of powdered sugar, and twelve lady fingers beaten into a powder. Beat the sugar with the eggs thoroughly, add the lady fingers and vanilla to taste. To be served in small glasses or cups.

STRAWBERRY CHARLOTTE

Make a boiled custard of one quart of milk, the yolks of six eggs and ¾ of a cup of sugar; flavor to taste. Line a glass fruit-dish with slices of sponge cake dipped in sweet cream; lay upon this ripe strawberries sweetened to taste; then a layer of cake and strawberries as before. When the custard is cold, pour over the whole. Now beat the whites of the eggs to a stiff froth, add a tbsp. of sugar to each egg and put over the top. Decorate the top with the largest berries saved out at the commencement. Raspberry Charlotte may be made the same way.

TIPSY CHARLOTTE

Take a stale sponge cake, cut the bottom and sides of it, so as to make it stand even in a glass fruit dish; make a few deep gashes through it with a sharp knife, pour over it a pint of good wine, let stand and soak into the cake. In the meantime, blanch, peel and slice lengthwise half a pound of sweet almonds; stick them all over the top of the cake. Have ready a pint of good boiled custard, well flavored, and pour over the whole. To be dished with a spoon. This is equally as good as any charlotte.

DESSERT PUFFS

Puffs for dessert are delicate and nice; take one pint of milk and cream each, the whites of four eggs beaten to a stiff froth, one heaping cupful of sifted flour, one scant cupful of powdered sugar, add a little grated lemon peel and a little salt; beat these all together till very light, bake in gem-pans, sift pulverized sugar over them and eat with sauce flavored with lemon.

STEWED APPLES

Apples cooked in the following way look very pretty on a tea-table and are appreciated by the palate. Select firm round greenings, pare neatly and cut in halves; place in a shallow stewpan with sufficient boiling water to cover them and a cup of sugar to every six apples. Each half should cook on the bottom of the pan and be removed from the others so as not to injure its shape. Stew slowly until the pieces are very tender; remove to a glass dish carefully, boil the syrup a half hour longer, pour it over the apples and eat cold. A few pieces of lemon boiled with the syrup add to the flavor.

CHOCOLATE MACROONS

Put three ounces of plain chocolate in a pan and melt on a slow fire; then work it to a thick paste with one pound of powdered sugar and the whites of three eggs; roll the mixture down to the thickness of about one-quarter of an inch; cut it in small, round pieces with a paste-cutter, either plain or scalloped; butter a pan slightly, and dust it with flour and sugar in equal quantities; place in it the pieces of paste or mixture, and bake in a hot but not too quick oven.

ICE CREAM

Genuine ice-cream is made of the pure sweet cream in this proportion: Two quarts of cream, one pound of sugar; beat up, flavor and freeze. The quantity, of course, can be increased to any amount desired so long as the relative proportions of the different ingredients are observed.

CHOCOLATE ICE CREAM

Add four ounces of grated chocolate to a cupful of sweet milk, then mix it thoroughly to a quart of thick sweet cream; no flavoring is required other than vanilla. Sweeten with a cupful of sugar; beat again and freeze.

CUSTARD ICE CREAM

Sweeten one quart of cream or rich milk with half a pound of sugar and flavor to taste; put it over the fire in a cereal kettle; as soon as it begins to boil, stir into it a tbsp. of cornstarch or rice flour which has been previously mixed smooth with a little milk; after it has boiled a few minutes, take it off the fire and stir in very gradually six eggs which have been beaten until thick; when quite cold, freeze it as ice cream.

RASPBERRY SHERBERT

Two quarts of raspberries, one cupful of sugar, 1½ pints of water, the juice of a large lemon, one tbsp. of gelatine. Mash the berries and sugar together and let them stand two hours. Soak the gelatine in cold water to cover. Add one pint of the water to the berries and strain. Dissolve the gelatine in half a pint of boiling water, add this to the strained mixture and freeze.

☆ ☆ ☆

TO HAVE A HAPPY LIFE

"It is not what we earn, as much as what we save, that makes us well-off. A long and happy life is the reward of obedience to nature's laws; and to be independent of want, is not to want what we do not need."

☆ ☆ ☆

Candy

CHOCOLATE CARAMELS

1 cup molasses
1 cup sugar
1 cup sweet milk
½ cup chocolate
¼ cup butter

Let boil until it forms a hard ball in cold water.

DIVINITY FUDGE

2 cup sugar
½ cup boiling water
½ cup corn syrup
Whites of two eggs

Boil until it snaps in cold water, beat the whites of egg very light, turn the boiling syrup into eggs. Beat until very creamy, add 1 cup chopped nuts and 1 tsp. vanilla, cut in squares while warm.

SUGARPLUMS

Handed down for many generations

16 oz. seedless raisins
11 oz. dried mixed fruit
Sugar
11 oz. dried figs or pitted prunes
1½ cups chopped walnuts

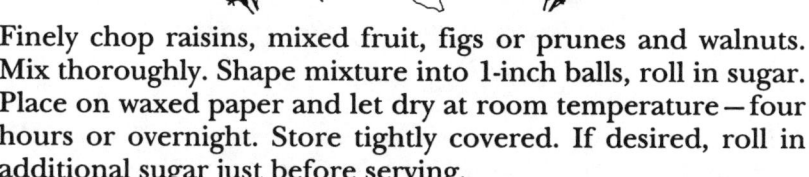

Finely chop raisins, mixed fruit, figs or prunes and walnuts. Mix thoroughly. Shape mixture into 1-inch balls, roll in sugar. Place on waxed paper and let dry at room temperature — four hours or overnight. Store tightly covered. If desired, roll in additional sugar just before serving.

FRUIT FUDGE
1850

3 cups sugar
3 tsp. cocoa
¼ cup coconut (grated)
¼ cup dried figs (chopped
¼ cup raisins

¾ cup milk
Butter the size of an egg
1 cup pecans (chopped)
¼ cup dates (chopped)

Boil sugar, cocoa, butter and milk until it forms a soft ball in cool water. Add fruit, mix well and turn into buttered dish. When nearly cold, cut into squares.

BUTTERSCOTCH CANDY

Great-grandmother Elsie K. Nagel made this candy, and it is a special treat to many of the older people.

1 cup sugar
4 tbsp. molasses
1 tbsp. vinegar

2 tbsp. boiling water
½ cup butter

Stir the ingredients and cook without stirring to the hard-crack stage (when the syrup is dropped in cold water, it breaks between the fingers if you try to crush it.) Turn into a large buttered tin, making a thin layer. When partly cool, mark in squares, or when cold break in pieces with the handle of a knife. Nutmeats may be added.

CHRISTMAS PUDDING CANDY

ca. 1880

This recipe is very old. The children would eat it all before Christmas if it wasn't hidden. So the rolls were hidden in different places, and one year a roll was lost until March when Carmen Hardt Miller found it. She said it was delicious!

3 cups sugar	1 tsp. vanilla
1 heaping tbsp. butter	1 cup light cream or milk
1 or 2 cups pecans	1 lb. figs
1 lb. dates	1 lb. coconut
1 lb. raisins	

Cook sugar, cream and butter to soft ball stage. Beat until creamy, then beat in fruit that is finely chopped. Mixed candied fruit may be used for part of fruit. Add nuts and vanilla. When well mixed, roll into logs and wrap in dampened cloth until cool. Remove from cloth; wrap in brown paper and put away to ripen. Make at least two weeks before you wish to use it. The longer it ages the better.

CHEWY CANDY

Rachel Jane Carson Underwood, 1860

1 cup grated chocolate	½ cup butter
½ cup milk	1½ cup molasses
1½ cup sugar	

Let cook until soft ball forms in cold water. Pour into medium size buttered pan. Cut into squares.

CHEWY MEXICAN PECAN PRALINES

Used on the farm outside Lockhart, Texas, by Lel Red Purcell who was born in 1859 in Gay Hill. There were over 300 pecan trees on the farm and Lel used them a lot when cooking.

2 cups white corn syrup
1½ cups granulated sugar
1 cup buttermilk
¼ lb. butter or lard
1 tsp. salt
1 tsp. baking soda
1 tsp. vanilla
2½-3 cups chopped pecans

Cook all ingredients except pecans, butter, and vanilla in a large heavy saucepan until very thick and sticky and makes a very hard ball (test in cold water). Remove from heat, add butter, pecans and vanilla. Beat until glossy. Spread in 2 buttered pans 13" x 9". Cool. Cut in squares and wrap.

MEXICAN CANDY
Katie Thornton, 1891

Take enough milk or water to moisten two pints of brown sugar (about ½ cup). When nearly boiled, put in a tbsp. of vinegar; then stir in the pecans (not quite half a pound), until it sugars. Pour out in little cakes on a cold piece of marble.

DIVINITY

2 cups sugar
½ cup light corn syrup
½ cups water
⅛ tsp. salt
2 egg whites
1 tsp. vanilla
⅔ cup pecans, chopped

Combine the sugar, corn syrup, water and salt in a qt. size saucepan. Cook over low heat until the sugar is dissolved, stirring continuously. Then cook without stirring to a firm ball stage, beat the egg whites until stiff but not dry. Wipe the crystals from the pouring edge of the pan with a damp cloth. Pour the syrup slowly, in a fine stream over the egg whites, beating constantly. While pouring, keep on beating until mixture

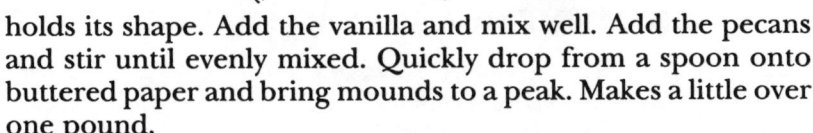

holds its shape. Add the vanilla and mix well. Add the pecans and stir until evenly mixed. Quickly drop from a spoon onto buttered paper and bring mounds to a peak. Makes a little over one pound.

Variations: (1) Add candied cherries to mixture with pecans. (2) Use other nuts in place of pecans. (3) Use 1 cup of brown sugar for 1 cup of white sugar. *Note:* Do not scrape the bottom of the pan after pouring the syrup over the egg whites. Store candy in an air tight container, between sheets of paper.

CHOCOLATE DROPS
Katie Thornton

Mix 2½ cups of sifted sugar with ½ cup of water, and boil hard for three or four minutes. Stir into it two tsp. of vanilla, take it off the fire, and stir quickly till it begins to be white and hard; then roll into little balls and put them on a greased pan, and when perfectly hard they must be covered with grated chocolate, which has been placed over the steam of the teakettle a few seconds until dissolved.

FONDANT FOR CANDY

2 cups sugar, 1 cup milk or 9 tbsp. water with a pinch of cream of tartar. Let boil until forms hairs from spoon. Let stand in cold water until a hole can be made without filling up. Beat until very creamy; then work with hands into small balls for candy.

PEPPERMINT DROPS
ca. 1900

1 cupful of sugar, ½ tsp. of essence of peppermint, a pinch of cream of tartar. Crush the sugar very fine, and boil for five minutes with water just sufficient to moisten. Then take from the fire and add the cream of tartar, and after mixing well add

the essence of peppermint. Beat briskly until the mixture begins to whiten well, and then drop upon white paper and dry in the open air. If it sugars before all is dropped, add a little water and boil again for two minutes.

MOLASSES CANDY
Eula Day, 1891

One pint molasses, one cup sugar. Boil, and stir every minute. When partly cooked put in ½ tsp. of butter. When it hardens in cold water it is done. Put in ½ tsp. cream of tartar with the butter, and just before you turn it out, put in a scant tsp. of soda.

CRYSTALLIZED ROSE PETALS

1 lb. of rose petals   1 lb. of sugar

Select beautiful red or pink rose petals that have been freshly gathered. Pick the petals one by one from the flowers, and put them into water. Drain this off, and then squeeze the flowers with your hands to bruise them, and drain on a sieve. Make a fine syrup, equal in bulk to the flowers, clarify it, and add the flowers. Let the syrup boil up about seven times. Then remove it from the fire and let it stand till the sugar forms a coating all around the petals. Then drain them, separate them on a paper for an hour or so, till perfectly dry, and then put in boxes lined with white paper, and keep in a cool, dry place.

CREAM PEANUTS

1 lb. of fine white sugar   1 tsp. extract of vanilla
1 teacupful Water   ½ lb. peanuts, shelled

Boil the sugar and water till it comes to a thread. Flavor highly with extract of vanilla. Then take from the fire and stir until it is a creamy white. Throw in the peanuts. Drop in a little white granulated sugar. Then put them on a table on a piece of white paper, and shake well till each stands apart. Roll again lightly in white powdered or granulated sugar, and let them dry.

PEANUT PRALINES

1 lb. peanuts	4 tbsp. water
1 lb. brown sugar	1 tbsp. butter

Shell the peanuts and break into bits. Then set the sugar water to boil, and as it begins to simmer add the peanuts and the butter. Stir constantly and as it bubbles up once take from the fire, pour from the spoon on the marble slab or a buttered plate, and set away to harden.

DATE LOAF
1885

Boil two cups sugar, ¾ cup milk until mixed, add one package of dates, stir well until candied. Remove from stove and beat well adding one cup of nuts.

Pour out on wet cloth and roll for a few minutes, then remove cloth and reroll. Let cool and slice like jelly roll.

DATE LOAF CANDY

This is our mother, Wanda Nowotny Streuer's, recipe. She always made it at Christmas Time and for other special occasions.

2 cups sugar	¼ cup butter
1 cup sweet milk	2 cups chopped pecans
1 lb. dates, pitted and chopped fine	1 tsp. vanilla

In a saucepan combine sugar and milk. Cook until mixture forms a soft ball in cold water. Add dates and beat until creamy. Add pecans, butter and vanilla and continue beating. Now pour mixture on a slightly damp kitchen towel and roll into a log shape. Wrap log (in foil) and chill. When ready to serve, slice in ½" slices. A delicious confection. *Note:* Roll the log about 1" in diameter.

ACTION OF SUGAR OR CANDY ON THE TEETH
1900

M. Larez, of France, in the course of his investigations on the teeth, has arrived at the following conclusions: First. That refined sugar, either from cane or beet, is injurious to healthy teeth, either by immediate contact with these organs, or by the gas developed owing to its seepage in the stomach. Second. That if a tooth is macerated in a saturated solution of sugar, it is so much altered in the chemical composition that it becomes gelatinous, and its enamel opaque, spongy, and easily broken. This modification is due, not to free acid, but to a tendency of sugar to combine with the calcareous basis of the teeth ... What say our candy-eating gentry to the above?

Canning and Pickling

CORN SALAT
Jean Haller, Republic of Texas

15 ears corn (about 10 cups cut off)	6 large onions
6 green tomatoes	6 ripe tomatoes
4 sweet peppers	4 hot peppers
1 head cabbage	3 pints vinegar
3 pints sugar	Salt and pepper to taste

Chop vegetables, mix all ingredients together and cook until done. Pour into sterilized jars and seal.

SWEET PICKLED CUCUMBER RINGS

Select large firm cucumbers (may use ripe, yellow ones). Pare and slice ½-inch thick, remove core carefully. Be sure to remove all soft part of core. For 1½ gallons of rings, soak overnight in cold water in which soda (2 tsp. to 1 gallon of water) is dissolved. Weight down with plate to keep rings covered by water. Next morning, drain and cover with water in which 4 scant tsp. of alum has been dissolved; again soak overnight. Next morning, drain alum water into enamel pot, bring to a boil, drop in cucumbers and boil 10 minutes. Drain cover with water in which 2 teaspoons powdered ginger has been dissolved.

Soak overnight, in morning, drain ginger water into pot, bring to a boil, add cucumbers and boil 15 minutes. While boiling, make a syrup of 1 quart vinegar, 6 cups sugar, ⅛ cup cinnamon bark and ⅛ cup whole cloves. Bring to a boil and add drained cucumbers. Boil until cucumbers are clear, pack into hot boiled fruit jars and seal immediately. They taste better if chilled before serving.

OCHRA AND TOMATOES

Take an equal quantity of each, let the ochra be young, slice it, skin the tomatoes; put them into a pan without water, add a lump of butter, an onion chopped fine, some pepper and salt, and stew them one hour.

TOMATO PASTE

Take one peck of ripe tomatoes and cook without water until they are tender. Put through a sieve, return to the fire and boil until thick. Stir constantly to prevent burning. Now add a pound of sugar, a half tsp. of salt, and pint of vinegar; and two tsp. of pepper. Boil again until thick. Pour into hot boiled bottles and seal or cork tightly.

GREEN TOMATO CATSUP

One peck of green tomatoes and two large onions sliced. Place them in layers, sprinkling salt between; let them stand twenty-four hours and then drain them. Add a quarter of a pound of mustard seed, one ounce allspice, one ounce cloves, one ounce ground mustard, one ounce ground ginger, two tbsp. black pepper, two tsp. celery seed, a quarter of a pound of brown sugar. Put all in preserving-pan, cover with vinegar and boil two hours; then strain through a sieve and bottle for use.

CUCUMBER CATSUP

Take cucumbers suitable for the table; peel and grate them, salt a little, and put in a bag to drain over night; in the morning season to taste with salt, pepper and vinegar, put in small jars and seal tight for fall or winter use.

APPLE CATSUP

Peel and quarter a dozen sound, tart apples; stew them until soft in as little water as possible, then pass them through a sieve. To a quart of the sifted apple, add a teacupful of sugar, one tsp. of pepper, one of cloves, one of mustard, two of cinnamon, and two medium-sized onions, chopped very fine. Stir all together adding a tbsp. of salt and a pint of vinegar. Place over the fire and boil one hour, and bottle while hot; seal very tight. It should be about as thick as tomato catsup, so that it will just run from the bottle.

GREEN TOMATO PICKLES (SWEET)

One peck of green tomatoes, sliced the day before you are ready for pickling, sprinkling them through and through with salt, not too heavily; in the morning drain off the liquor that will drain from them. Have a dozen good-sized onions rather coarsely sliced; take a suitable kettle and put in a layer of the sliced tomatoes, then of onions, and between each layer sprinkle the following spices; six red peppers chopped coarsely, one cup of sugar, one tbsp. of ground allspice, one tbsp. of ground cinnamon, a tsp. of cloves, one tbsp. of mustard. Turn over three pints of good vinegar, or enough to completely cover them; boil until tender. This is a choice recipe.

If the flavor of onions is objectionable, the pickle is equally as good without them.

PICKLED CABBAGE

Cut a sound cabbage into quarters, spread it on a large flat platter or dish and sprinkle thickly with salt; set it in a cool place for twenty-four hours, and cover with cold vinegar for twelve hours. Prepare a pickle by seasoning with enough vinegar to cover the cabbage with equal quantities of mace, allspice, cinnamon and black pepper, a cup of sugar to every gallon of vinegar, and a tsp. of celery seed to every pint. Pack the cabbage in a stone jar; boil the vinegar and spices five minutes and pour on hot. Cover and set away in a cool, dry place. It will be good in a month. A few slices of beet-root improves the color.

PEPPER MANGOES
Mrs. G. S. Criser, 1891

Take the cap out of the pepper mango's pod, then scrape out the seed, lay the pods in salt water for an hour. Chop cabbage very fine, and to every quart, add one tbsp. of salt, one tbsp. of ground black pepper, two tbsp. of white mustard seed, one tbsp. of cloves, one of cinnamon and one cup of sugar. Mix all together. Drain the pepper pods and stuff them with the mixture, replace the caps, pack them closely in a stone jar, then pour on them strong vinegar. Then they are ready for use in a few weeks.

PICKLED ONIONS

Peel small onions until they are white. Scald them in salt and water until tender, then take them up, put them into wide-mouthed bottles, and pour over them hot spiced vinegar; when cold, cork them closed. Keep in a dry, dark place. A tbsp. of sweet oil may be put in the bottles before the cork. The best sort of onions for pickling are the small white buttons.

CHOW CHOW
1899

1 small head of cabbage
1 gallon green tomatoes
1 cup of sugar
1 tsp. ground cinnamon
1 tsp. of mustard
1 tsp. of ground cloves
½ dozen peppers
   (green or ripe)
2 large onions

Chop tomatoes and cabbage and sprinkle with ½ cup of salt; mix well; let stand over night. Next morning drain off the water; then add onions, peppers and seasoning and run through a meat mill. Put in a granite vessel, cover with vinegar, and boil about 1 hour. Put in Mason jars and seal.

CHOW CHOW
Minnie Gilmore Lee

4 cups ground onions
4 cups ground cabbage
4 cups ground green peppers
4 cups ground green tomatos
12 hot chili peppers
½ cup salt
1 recipe preserving syrup

Mix ground or finely chopped vegetables; cover with water to which the salt has been added. Let stand overnight or 12 hours. Chill if possible. Drain vegetables thoroughly, using cheesecloth, for about 30 minutes. Add syrup, cook 45 minutes to 1 hour. Pour into sterilized jars and seal.

Preserving Syrup:
1 cup sugar
1 tbsp. celery seed
2 tbsp. mustard seed
1½ tsp. turmeric
1 qt. cider vinegar

Mix ingredients and bring to a boil; add vegetables.

PICKLED BEETS
Great-grandmother Minnie Gilmore Lee

Wash beets and cut off tops. Cook until tender, remove skins. Slice ¼-inch thick. Pack into hot sterilized jars, cover with hot vinegar, to which 1 tsp. pickling spice and ½ tsp. salt has been added; add ½ cup sugar, 1 cup of water, boil.

AN ORNAMENTAL PICKLE

Boil fresh eggs half an hour, then put them in cold water. Boil red beets until tender, peel and cut in dice form, cover with vinegar, spiced; shell the eggs and drop into the pickle jar.

MIXED PICKLES

Scald in salt water until tender cauliflower heads, small onions, peppers, cucumbers cut in dice, nasturtiums and green beans; then drain until dry and pack into wide-mouthed bottles.

    Boil in each a pint of cider vinegar, one tbsp. of sugar, half a tsp. of salt and two tbsp. of mustard; pour over the pickle and seal carefully. Other spices may be added if liked.

CHOPPED PICKLES
Mrs. G. S. Criser, 1891

One peck green tomatoes, twelve green peppers, one head of cabbage, ½ dozen ripe cucumbers, ½ dozen green cucumbers, six large onions, two heads of celery, all chopped fine, and mix with one teacup of coarse salt. Let stand twelve hours; drain perfectly dry, and scald thoroughly in two quarts of vinegar. Drain and pack in jars. When cold, pour over two quarts of vinegar to which has been added ½ cup of grated horse radish, one tbsp. of ground mace, one tbsp. each of ground cinnamon, allspice, mustard and cayenne pepper, ½ oz. each of celery seed and mustard seed, three cups of sugar. Cover with plate to keep under vinegar. Cover closely the top with thick cloth.

YELLOW PICKLE
Mrs. Ed. Wayland, 1891

Yellow pickle made three years old in three hours: After cucumbers, cauliflowers, or cabbage have been in brine, soak nearly all the salt out and boil them in weak vinegar. Take them out of the vinegar. Then boil for ten minutes a gallon of strong vinegar into which put two lbs. sugar, two tbsp. of crushed celery seed, two tbsp. of allspice, two tbsp. of ginger, one tsp. of mace, and one tsp. of cloves. Put a gallon of pickles in a jar, and pour this boiling vinegar over them, when cold add six whole onions, three tbsp. of turmeric, and three of grated or sliced horse radish. All the spices ought to be crushed before being boiled in vinegar.

SPICED PLUMS

Seven lbs. of plums, one pint of cider vinegar, four lbs. of sugar, two tbsp. of broken cinnamon bark, half as much of whole cloves and the same of broken nutmeg; place these in a muslin bag and simmer them in a little vinegar and water for half an hour; then add it all to the vinegar and sugar, and bring to a boil; add the plums and boil carefully until they are cooked tender. Before cooking the plums they should be pierced with a darning needle several times; this will prevent the skins bursting while cooking.

PEACH OR PLUM SWEET PICKLES
1899

Three lbs. of fruit, 1 lb. sugar, 1 qt. of vinegar, spice to taste. Boil sugar and vinegar together and put in fruit, boil until thick enough to keep.

SWEET PICKLE PEACHES
Mrs. J. I. Vredenburgh, 1891

To every 10 lbs. of pared peaches, allow 4½ lbs. of sugar, and one qt. of vinegar. Place the sugar over the fire, with about a half teacup of water to every 4½ lbs. of sugar. Boil and skim. Put in the fruit and boil five minutes, or until it can be pierced with a broom straw. Take out the fruit with a perforated skimmer and fill the fruit jars. Add the vinegar, and mace, stick cinnamon, and whole cloves to taste, to the syrup. Boil ten minutes longer and pour over the fruit in the jars; removing all air bubbles by carefully running a knife down to them. Fill the jars full to overflowing with the syrup and seal immediately. Cling stone peaches are the best for sweet pickle.

SPICED PEACHES
Mrs. Joseph Spence, 1891

One peck peaches, one gallon vinegar, seven lbs. brown sugar, ½ dozen whole cloves, ½ dozen sticks cinnamon broken into inch pieces. Boil the vinegar after putting in the sugar and spices; when it gets to boiling throw in as many peeled peaches as will cover the top of the kettle, and boil them until you can run a straw through them, and so on until all are done; fill the jars ¾ full and fill up with the vinegar and spices.

Household Hints

DISCLAIMER
The home remedies and household hints contained in this book are provided for historical purposes only. No express or implied warranties with regard to their efficacy or safety are made by the Daughters of the Republic of Texas, District VIII. Do not use them without first consulting a physician or other appropriate medical professional. Daughters of the Republic of Texas are not engaged in rendering medical advice.

☆ ☆ ☆

DECORATIONS FOR A PARTY DURING THE REPUBLIC OF TEXAS

The first Republic of Texas Capitol was a two-room log building divided by a hall. The senate chamber was the scene of many social, religious, and other gatherings. One affair that worked a miracle of beauty in the old hall was in honor of Colonel Martin and Francisco Peraza sent as envoys to Texas from Yucatan and Tabasco, while revolted from Mexico, to treat for the use of the small Texas Navy; they in part bearing the expenses of fighting the common enemy. The propositions were acceded to, and to honor the guests the accustomed ball in the Republic of Texas senate chamber was given.

"I can hardly express what a fairy land of flowers grew up under the wreathing touch of fair hands, aided by the strong hands of active young men. Bands of flowers, (Texas wild flowers), wreaths of flowers and mottoes of flowers, wreaths and single bright flowers, were suspended by gossamer threads, so as to look like fairy gifts descending. The resinous odor of cedar, mingled with that of the thousand flowers, was like a continued incense." [by Julia Lee sinks, who helped decorate and attended the ball. She later became a member of the Daughters of The Republic of Texas.]

☆ ☆ ☆

Toilet Recipes

ROSE WATER

Preferable to the distilled for a perfume, or for culinary purposes. Attar of rose, twelve drops; rub it up with half an ounce of white sugar and two drachms carbonate magnesia; then add gradually one quart of water and two ounces of proof spirit, and filter through paper.

JOCKEY CLUB BOUQUET

Mix one pint extract of rose, one pint extract of tuberose, half a pint of extract of cassia, four ounces extract of jasmine, and three ounces tincture of civet. Filter the mixture.

LAVENDER WATER

Oil of lavender two ounces, orris root half an ounce, spirits of wine one pint. Mix and keep two or three weeks. It may then be strained through two thicknesses of blotting-paper and is ready for use.

CREAM OF ROSES

Olive oil one pound, attar of roses fifty drops, oil of rosemary twenty-five drops; mix, and color it with alkanet root.

CREAM OF LILIES

Best white castor oil; pour in a little strong solution of sal tartar in water, and shake it until it looks thick and white. Perfume with lavender.

POWDER FOR THE FACE

Five cents' worth of bay rum, five cents' worth of magnesia snowflake, five cents' worth of bergamot, five cents' worth of oil of lemon; mix in a pint bottle and fill up with rain-water. Shake well, and apply with a soft sponge or cloth.

LIP SALVE
1865

Melt together 2½ ounces of white wax, 3 ounces of spermaceti, 7 ounces oil of almonds, 1 drachm of balsam of Pru, and 1½ ounces of glycerin wrapped up in a linen bag.

Pour the salve into small gallipots or boxes, and cover with bladder and white leather

OXMARROW-POMADE FOR THE HAIR

One marrow bone, half a pint of oil, ten cents' worth of citronella. Take the marrow out of the bone, place it in warm water, let it get almost to boiling point, then let it cool and pour the water away; repeat this three times until the marrow is thoroughly "fined." Beat the marrow to a cream with a silver fork, stir the oil in, drop by drop, beating all the time; when quite cold add the citronella, pour into jars and cover down.

TO INCREASE THE HAIR IN THE BROWS

Clip them and anoint with a little sweet oil. Should the hair fall out, having been full, use one of the hair invigorators.

COLD CREAM

Melt one ounce oil of almonds, half ounce spermaceti, one drachm white wax, and then add two ounces of rose-water, and stir it constantly until cold.

HAIR DYE

There is danger in some of the patent hair dyes, and hence the *Scientific American* offers what is known as the walnut hair dye. The simplest form is the expressed juice of the bark or shell of green walnuts. To preserve the juice a little alcohol is commonly added to it with a few bruised cloves, and the whole "digested" together, with occasional agitation, for a week or

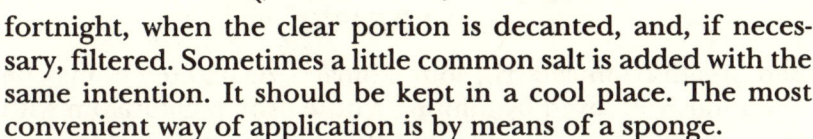

fortnight, when the clear portion is decanted, and, if necessary, filtered. Sometimes a little common salt is added with the same intention. It should be kept in a cool place. The most convenient way of application is by means of a sponge.

HAIR WASH

One penny's worth of borax, half a pint of olive oil, one pint of boiling water. Pour the boiling water over the borax and oil; let it cool; then put the mixture into a bottle. Shake it before using, and apply it with a flannel.

Camphor and borax, dissolved in boiling water and left to cool, make a very good wash for the hair; as also does rosemary water mixed with a little borax. After using any of these washes, when the hair becomes thoroughly dry, a little pomatum or oil should be rubbed in to make it smooth and glossy — that is, if one prefers oil on the hair.

TO REMOVE FRECKLES

One ounce of lemon juice, a quarter of a drachm of powdered borax, and half a drachm of sugar; mix in a bottle, and allow them to stand a few days, when the liquor should be rubbed occasionally on the hands and face.

A tbsp. of freshly grated horse-radish, stirred into a cupful of sour milk; let it stand for twelve hours, then strain and apply often. This bleaches the complexion also, and takes off tan.

TO REMOVE MOTH PATCHES

Into a pint of rum put a tbsp. of flour of sulphur. Apply this to the patches once a day, and they will disappear in two or three weeks.

TOOTH POWDER

Prepared chalk half a pound, powdered myrrh, two ounces; camphor, two drachms; orris root, powdered, two ounces; moisten the camphor with alcohol and mix well together.

BAD BREATH

Bad breath from catarrh, sour stomach, or bad teeth, may be temporarily relieved by diluting a little bromo chloralum with eight or ten parts of water, and using it as a gargle, and swallowing a few drops before going out. A pint of bromo chloralum costs fifty cents, but a small vial will last a long time.

RAZOR-STROP PASTE

Wet the strop with a little sweet oil, and apply a little flour of emery evenly over the surface.

BANDOLINE

To one quart of rose-water add an ounce and a half of gum tragacanth; let it stand forty-eight hours, frequently straining it, then strain through a coarse linen cloth; let it stand two days, and again strain; add to it a drachm of oil of roses. Used by ladies dressing their hair, to make it lie in any position.

Care of Clothing

TO CLEAN BLACK LACE, NO. 1

A tsp. of gumaraic dissolved in one teacupful of boiling water; when cool, add half a tsp. of black ink; dip the lace and spread smoothly between the folds of a newspaper and press dry with book or the like. Lace shawls can be pressed over in this way, by pinning a sheet to the carpet and stretching the shawl upon that; or black lace can be cleaned the same as ribbon and silk. Take an old kid glove (black preferable), no matter how old, and boil it in a pint of water for a short time; then let it cool until the leather can be taken in hand without burning; use the glove to sponge off the ribbon; if the ribbon is very dirty, dip it into water and draw through the fingers a few times before sponging. After cleaning, lay a piece of paper over the ribbon and iron; paper is better than cloth. The ribbon will look like new.

TO CLEAN BLACK LACE, NO. 2

Black laces of all kinds may be cleaned by alcohol. Throw them boldly into the liquid; churn them up and down till they foam; if very dusty, use the second dose of alcohol; squeeze them out, "spat" them, pull out the edges, lay them between brown paper, smooth and straight; leave under a heavy weight till dry; do not iron.

TO REMOVE PAINT FROM BLACK SILK

Patient rubbing with chloroform will remove paint from black silk or any other goods, and will not hurt the most delicate color or fabric.

TO WASH WHITE THREAD LACE

To wash white lace, cover a bottle with linen, stitched smoothly to fit the shape. Wind the lace about it, basting both edges to the linen. Wash on the bottle, soaping and rinsing well, then boil in soft water. Dry in the sun. Clip the basting threads and do not iron. If carefully done, it will look like new lace.

NOVEL DRESS MENDING

A novel way of mending a woolen or silk dress in which a round hole has been torn, and where only a patch could remedy matters, is the following: The frayed portions around the tear should be carefully smoothed, and a piece of the material, moistened with very thin muscilage, placed under the hole. A heavy weight should be put upon it until it is dry, when it is only possible to discover the mended place by careful observation.

POLISH OR ENAMEL FOR SHIRTWAISTS

Melt together one ounce of white wax, and two ounces of spermaceti; heat gently and turn into a very shallow pan; when cold cut or break in pieces. When making boiled starch the usual way, enough for a dozen bosoms, add to it a piece of the polish the size of a hazel nut.

TO DYE STRAW BONNETS BROWN
1865

Take a sufficient quantity of Brazil-wood, sumach, bark, madder, copperas, and sadden, according to the shade required.

CLOTHES THAT HAVE A BAD ODOR

Clothes which have a bad odor may be wrapped up and buried for a day or two in the ground to remove the odor.

School and Home Aids

GLUE AND CEMENT
1899

Glue to resist heat and moisture is made as follows: Mix a handful of quick-lime in four ounces of linseed oil, boil to a good thickness, then spread it on tin plates in the shade, and it will become very hard, but may be easily be dissolved over the fire as glue.

Glue which will resist the action of water is made by boiling one pound of common glue in two quarts of skimmed milk.

1877

To attach metal to glass mix two ounces of a thick solution of glue with one ounce of linseed-oil varnish, and half an ounce of pure spirits of turpentine; boil the whole together in a close vessel. After it has been applied to the glass and metal, clamp together for two or three days, until dry.

Cement for mending almost any thing, may be made by mixing litharge and glycerine to the consistency of thick cream or fresh putty. This cement is useful for mending stone jars, stopping leaks in seams of tin pans or wash-boilers, cracks in iron kettles. Do not use mended article until the cement has hardened.

PASTE

Lel Red Purcell used this paste in her school, Stuart Seminary, (1876–1899), in Austin, Texas; her granddaughter Lel used the same recipe when teaching kindergarten many years later.

"Perpetual" paste may be made by dissolving a tsp. of alum in a quart of water. When cold, stir in as much flour as will give it the consistency of thick cream, being particular to beat up all the lumps; stir in as much powdered rosin as will lay on a five-cent piece, and throw in half a dozen cloves to give it a pleasant odor. Have on the fire a tea-cupful of boiling water, pour the flour mixture into it, stirring well at the time. In a few minutes it will be of the consistency of mush. Pour it into an earthen vessel, let it cool, lay a cover on, and put in a cool place. When needed for use, take out a portion and soften it with warm water. Paste made in this way will last a year. It is better than gum, as it does not gloss the paper which can be written upon.

TO MAKE TRACING PAPER

Dissolve a ball of white beeswax, one inch in diameter, in half a pint of turpentine. Saturate the paper in this bath and let it dry two or three days before using.

Creepy Crawly Things

TROUBLESOME ANTS

A heavy chalk mark laid a finger's distance from your sugar box and all around (there must be no space not covered) will surely prevent ants from troubling.

COCKROACHES DESTROYED

Sprinkle the floor with hellebore at night. The roaches consume it and are poisoned.
    Sprinkle Scotch snuff in the hole where they come out.

FLEAS

Sprinkle about the bed a few drops of oil of lavender to drive off fleas.

Household Maintenance

AN ERASIVE FLUID FOR THE REMOVAL OF SPOTS ON FURNITURE OR FABRICS WITHOUT INJURING THE COLOR

Four ounces of aqua ammonia, one ounce of glycerine, one ounce of castile soap and one of spirits of wine. Dissolve the soap in two quarts of soft water, add the other ingredients. Apply with a soft sponge and rub out. Very good for cleaning silks.

TO VENTILATE A ROOM

Place a pitcher of cold water on a table in your room and it will absorb all the gases with which the room is filled from the respiration of those eating or sleeping in the apartment. Very few realize how important such purification is for the health of the family or, indeed, understand or realize that there can be any impurity in the rooms; yet in a few hours a pitcher or pail of cold water—the colder the more effective—will make the air of a room pure, but the water will be entirely fit for use.

TALLOW CANDLES FOR SUMMER USE

Most tallow, in summer, is more or less soft, and often quite yellow. To avoid both: Take your tallow and put a little beeswax with it, especially if adding weak lye, and gently boil an hour or two each day for 2 days, stirring and skimming well; each morning cutting it out and scraping off the bottom which is soft, adding fresh lye (be sure it is not too strong), 1, or 2, or 3 gals., according to the amount of tallow. The third morning use water in which alum and saltpetre are dissolved, at the rate

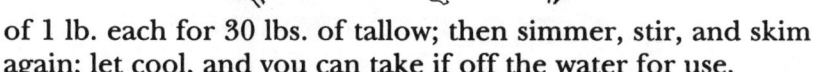

of 1 lb. each for 30 lbs. of tallow; then simmer, stir, and skim again; let cool, and you can take if off the water for use.

They may be dipped or run in moulds. For dipping allow two pounds for each dozen candles.

Saltpetre and alum are said to harden lard for candles; but it can be placed among the humbugs of the day.

AN AGREEABLE DISINFECTANT

Sprinkle fresh ground coffee on a shovel of hot coals, or burn sugar on hot coals. Vinegar boiled with myrrh, sprinkled on the floor and furniture of a sick room, is an excellent deodorizer.

TO MEND SHEETS

When sheets are beginning to wear in the middle, sew the selvages sides together and rip open the old seam, or tear in two and hem the sides.

TO PREVENT CREAKING OF BEDSTEADS

If a bedstead creaks at each movement of the sleeper, remove the slats, and wrap the ends of each in old newspapers.

CREAKING HINGE'S PREVENTED

Rub hinges with a feather dipped in oil.

LEAD PIPES

Never use water which has stood in a lead pipe over night. Not less than a wooden bucketful should be allowed to run before using the water.

TO PICK UP BROKEN GLASS

Small pieces of broken glassware may be picked up from the floor or other hard surfaces with dampened, absorbent cotton.

CARE OF KITCHEN SINK

When the dish washing is completed, wash every part of the sink with hot, soapy water or scour. Wash above and around the sink. Use a skewer to clean behind the sink pipes. Flush the sink with boiling water every day and about once a week with a strong solution of washing soda.

TO WASH DISHES

Have a pan half-filled with hot soapy water. Slip glasses and fine china in sideways, that the hot water will touch outside and inside at the same time, and thus avoid danger of cracking. If dishes are very greasy, add a little washing soda, or ammonia. Rinse all dishes in clean hot water, (except cut glass) drain and wipe with clean, dry towel.

REMOVAL OF GREASE FROM FLOOR

When grease drops on the floor, pour ice cold water on it immediately to harden the grease so it will not soak into the wood.

TO CLEAN FURNITURE

To clean furniture take a large cotton rag well saturated with coal oil, rub each article of furniture with it until all the mud-stains and dust have disappeared, then go over it with a dry cloth, rubbing each piece until it is perfectly dry. Clean once a week.

FOOD KEEPER

Before the days of refrigerators and ice boxes was the covered cabinet. It was about two feet square and about six feet tall with about three shelves in it. It was an open frame work with 2" x 2" part at each corner and cleats for the shelves to rest upon. A full length door was hinged on one side. The whole thing was covered with a mosquito netting. A very large bowl was placed on top of the cabinet. The mosquito netting was then placed over the bowl and draped down the sides to cover the cabinet. A large heavy rock was placed in the bowl to hold the netting. Water was then placed in the bowl and would siphon over the edge and seep down to keep it damp. The cabinet was placed in an open hallway or on a porch in a shady spot. The air passing through this damp netting kept the food stuff nice and cool and also kept the flies away from the food.

TO CLEAN CARPETS AND RUGS

To clean carpets and rugs, sweep, wet a cloth with water to which a few spoonfuls of ammonia have been added, wring out the cloth and wipe carpet or rug.

CHEAP CARPET

Make a cover for the floor of the cheapest cotton cloth. Tack it down like a carpet, paper it as you would a wall with paper resembling a carpet in figures, let it dry, varnish with two coats of varnish and with reasonable usage it will last two years.

MAKE RAG RUGS

Cut rags and sew hit and miss, or fancy-striped as you choose; use wooden needles, round, smooth, and pointed at one end, of any convenient length. The knitting is done back and forth (like old fashioned suspenders), always taking off the first stitch.

TO LAY A CARPET

If put down well, carpet wears better. It is well to have it done by experienced persons when affordable. Put down coarse paper or newspapers evenly on the floor first; begin at one corner, and nail down one of the sides evenly on the floor first; at the cut ends of the breadths, continuing around the selvage side and stretching it evenly and firmly without straining the fabric. When two sides are nailed, take next the other selvage side. The last side will require the most stretching in order to get rid of puckers.

STAIR CARPETS

To make stair carpets wear longer place extra thicknesses of paper over the edge of each stair, the full width of the carpet, before fastening down the carpet.

TO MAKE GARDEN WALKS

Coal ashes make excellent garden walks. They become very hard by use and no weeds or grass will grow through them.

TO DESTROY WEEDS IN WALKS

To destroy weeds in walks boil ten pounds stone lime, five gallons water and one pound flour of sulphur, let settle, pour off clear part, and sprinkle freely upon the weedy walks.

TO MEND TIN

Scrape the tin about the hole free from grease and rust, rub on a piece of resin until a powder lies about the hole, over it lay a piece of solder, and hold on it a hot poker or soldering iron until it melts.

CESS POOLS DISINFECTED INSTANTLY
1887

Prof. Thos. Taylor reports that 1 tbsp. of spirits of turpentine in 1 pail of water will disinfect an ordinary cess pool instantly, and that in the sick chamber it will prove a powerful auxiliary against germs and bad odors. Note: I think, 2 or 3 spoonfuls to the pail of water would be equally effective for a water-closet—privy.

TO TEMPER LAMP CHIMNEYS

Lamp chimneys and glass-ware for hot water is made less liable to break by putting in cold water, bringing slowly to boiling point, boiling for an hour, and allowing to cool before removing from water.

MAGIC FURNITURE POLISH

The recipe for magic furniture polish: mix a half pint of alcohol, half ounce of resin, a half ounce of gum-shellac, a few drops of analine brown; let stand over night and add three-fourths pint raw linseed oil and half pint spirits of turpentine; shake well before using. Apply with cotton flannel cloth and rub dry with another cloth.

To Lighten the Washing Chores

SPOTS FROM WASH GOODS

Rub them with the yolk of egg before washing.

TO REMOVE INK, WINE, OR FRUIT STAINS

Saturate well in tomato juice; it is also an excellent thing to remove stains from the hands.

TO SET COLORS IN WASHABLE CLOTHES

Soak them previous to washing in a water in which is allowed a tbsp. of ox-gall to a gallon of water.

THE WEEKLY WASH
1800s

Much time can be saved in gathering the wash if a plain muslin bag for collecting laundry is hung on each closet door. Then each member of the family could be responsible for bringing his own laundry.

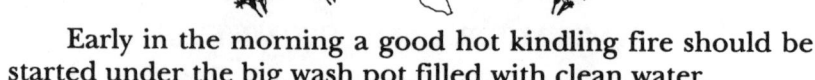

Early in the morning a good hot kindling fire should be started under the big wash pot filled with clean water.

Careful sorting of the clothes is important. The general wash in the large family may be sorted into six groups:

1. Fine white things such as table linens and fine white clothes.
2. Heavy white things such as bath towels and underwear.
3. Soiled white pieces — dish towels, hand towels, etc.
4. Light colored things — dresses, shirts.
5. Soiled colored things — children's play clothes, aprons, work shirts, etc.
6. "Last water" things — overalls, socks, dirty pants, rags.

It may be necessary to add soap and hot water from time to time. The first order of clothes goes into the hottest water. From the wash tub the clothes are wrung out and put in first rinse, then wrung out and then to last rinse which has a little amount of bluing added.

To keep clothes from freezing to the line in cold weather, wipe line with a rag wrung out of strong salt water.

When hanging out large pieces — sheets and tablecloths, pin all four corners to the line to prevent being whipped by the Texas wind.

After starching house dresses, wring them out. This takes out extra starch.

To keep clothes line props from slipping out from under the line, drive a long nail to part of its depth in the bottom of the pole. The nail sticks into the ground and prevents slipping.

To whiten linen when it looks gray, put four slices of lemon with rind in the water in which you boil the linen.

Hang socks on a fence loop over once to hold them.

The smell of air-dried clothes and firewood under the washout makes the work all worthwhile.

HOME MADE LYE SOAP

Save all your bacon grease in tins and strain.

Empty contents of one can of lye into 2½ pints of cold water in iron or enamel utensil. *[Our grandma used the old washpot.]*

Stir until dissolved and allow to cool.

Boil fat (in double its amount) in water. Skim off six pounds of clean grease. Pour lukewarm lye solution slowly into lukewarm grease, stirring thoroughly for 15 minutes. Pour into metal or glass pans, let set for three days, then cut into cakes.

TO RETAIN COLORS

To keep the colors of calico and gingham bright for a long time, dissolve a piece of alum the size of a hickory nut for every pint of starch and add to it. This will keep it bright a long time.

BLEACHING CLOTHES

A tsp. of turpentine boiled with white clothes will aid materially in the bleaching process.

TO PREVENT RUST ON FLAT IRONS

Beeswax and salt will make your rusty flat-irons as smooth and clean as glass. Tie a lump of wax in a rag and keep it for that purpose. When the irons are hot rub them first with the wax rag, then scour with a paper or cloth sprinkled with salt.

Child Care and Games

INFANT CARE, 1866

A child when born, should be laid for the first month upon a thin mattress which the nurse may sometimes keep on her knee, that the child may always lie, and only sit up as the nurse slants the mattress. Keep it as dry as possible. At the end of a month the nurse may set it up, and dance it by degrees.

The clothing should be light, and not much longer than itself, that the legs may be readily reached and rubbed, for rubbing takes off scurf, and causes the blood to circulate. Rubbing the ankle-bones and inside of the knees will strengthen those parts, and make the child stretch its knees, and keep them flat.

During the first fortnight the child should sleep on a bed, except when taken up to supply its wants, which will give it early habits of cleanliness. It is injurious to be laid always asleep on a person's knee.

The wisest course in treating infants, is to follow the simple dictates of nature; yet some people are so devoid of consideration as to give them wine, spirit, spices, sugar, and other things too strong for their tender stomachs.

Never expose the infant to open doors or windows, especially in winter. The extreme of a summer day should also be avoided. Excessive heat or cold will injure an infant. Infants should not be kept too near the fire.

In the latter part of the first year, pure water may occasionally be given. Those parents who accustom their children to drink water only, bestow on them a benefit, the value of which will be sensibly felt through life. Habits of intemperance, the curse of after life, are often lain in infancy.

QUEEN ANNE AND HER MAIDS

The players divide into two parties. One side takes a ball, and draw close together, raising frocks into a "lap" or cover, into which the players put their hands. The ball is given to a player to keep in her lap. She must try to hide it as much as possible, while those whose laps are empty must "make believe," as well as they can to hold the ball in their raised dresses. This done by pushing the dress out with the hand, etc. When the ball has been concealed, the players advance to those waiting on the other side of the room and sing:

> *Queen Anne, Queen Anne, she sat in the sun,*
> *As white as a lily, as grave as a nun;*
> *She sends you these letters, and begs you'll read one;*
> *If you guess our secret, 'twill be great fun."*

The other players answer:

> *Good fortune the gracious Queen befall,*
> *I ask Amelia [or whatever name may be] to give me the ball.*

If her guess is mistaken, the maids of honor sing:

> *The ball is ours; you guess not well,*
> *Nor can our lady's secret tell;*
> *So sit like gypsies in the sun,*
> *While we, fair ladies, go and come.*

Then they return to their places, and transfer the ball to another play-fellow.

When the guessers fix on the right person, the ball is transferred to them, and the parts are reversed, while the ball-holder has to pay a forfeit.

BUZZ

Promptness is very necessary in this game. Any number of children except seven, both girls and boys, seat themselves around a table, or in a circle. One begins the game by saying "One!" the child on the left says "Two!" and so on until they come to seven, which number must not be mentioned, but in place thereof the word "BUZZ!" Whenever a number occurs in which the figure seven is used, or any number into which seven may be multiplied, 17, 21, 27, 36, 37, 42, etc. Any one mentioning a number with seven in it instead of "BUZZ!" or calling out of turn, or naming a wrong number, must pay a forfeit. After she has paid her forfeit, she calls out "One!" and so it goes round again to the left. When by a little practice, the circle gets as high as seventy-one then "Buzz-one, Buzz-two", etc. must be used, and for seventy-seven, "Buzz-buzz" and so on. If the person whose turn it is to speak delays longer than while any one of the circle can moderately count five, she must pay a forfeit.

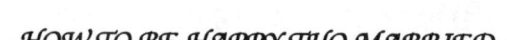

HOW TO BE HAPPY THO MARRIED

[A little treatise purports to contain the twelve pieces of advice given by a mother to her daughter on the eve of the latter's marriage.]

1. Avoid everything likely to annoy your husband. Don't appear gay if he is sad, or sad if he is gay.

2. Try to find out what dishes he likes, and if your taste does not accord with his, don't let him see it. In fact—feed the brute!

3. If your husband has dropt off to sleep through illness or weariness, take care not to wake him, and if you absolutely must, do it gently and do not make him start.

4. Be faithful in love, and do not rob your husband: don't give away or lend his possessions without his permission.

5. Don't appear too anxious to know your husband's affairs, but if he does tell you about them, keep his secrets and never repeat in public things told you in private, however trivial they may appear.

6. Love your family, especially those whom your husband loves, and don't find fault with them for little things.

7. Don't do anything of any importance without asking your husband's advice and always consider what he says to be best.

8. Don't make impossible or wrong demands upon him, which displease him and are contrary to his honor, so that no evil may come upon him through you.

9. Be careful always to look pretty and neat. Be suitably drest without ostentation or exaggeration, for if you wear fast clothes your husband will think you are fast.

10. Don't be too familiar with your servants. It makes them scornful and disrespectful.

11. Don't want to go out too often. Man's sphere is outside; the sphere of woman is the home. Speak seldom, be modest, and don't frequent fortune tellers.

12. Finally, and most important of all, do nothing which could possibly make your husband jealous, for thus you will lose his love. When he comes home, receive him with pleasure. Make much of him, and pay more attention to his relatives than to your own, and then he will act in the same way toward you. See that everything in your home runs smoothly. And always make yourself attractive.

☆   ☆   ☆

Home Remedies

DISCLAIMER
The home remedies and household hints contained in this book are provided for historical purposes only. No express or implied warranties with regard to their efficacy or safety are made by the Daughters of the Republic of Texas, District VIII. Do not use them without first consulting a physician or other appropriate medical professional. Daughters of the Republic of Texas are not engaged in rendering medical advice.

Home remedies' recipes were passed from mouth to mouth and swapped by pioneer women wherever they met, on frontier ranches, in towns, at camp meetings and on the trails to the southwest. The pioneer women were the "nurses and doctors" of their families. It is impossible to trace a home remedy to its source.

Some folk medicine "cures" were based on superstition.

TO KEEP THE FEET DRY

One method has been found to succeed in keeping the feet dry is to wear, over the foot of the stocking, a sock made of oiled silk. To keep it in its proper place, it will be necessary to wear over it a cotton or worsted sock. India-rubber overshoes of boots are now generally worn. But they or oiled silk, are not desirable as they prevent the evaporation of the insensible perspiration, and thus obstruct the pores of the skin, should never be worn long at a time.

CERATE OF SPANISH FLY

Take of cerate of spermaceti, softened with heat, 6 drachms; Spanish flies, finely powdered, 1 drachms; Mix them by melting over a gentle fire.

Under this form cantharides may be made to act to any extent that is requisite. It may supply the place either of the blistering plaster or ointment, and there are cases in which it is preferable to either. It is particularly more convenient than the plaster of cantharides, where the skin to which the blister is to be applied is previously much affected, as in cases of small-pox, and in supporting a drain under the tissue as it is less apt to spread than the softer ointment.

CURE FOR PIMPLES

One tsp. of carbolic acid and one pint of rose-water mixed is an excellent remedy for pimples. Bathe the skin thoroughly and often, but do not let the wash get into the eyes. This wash is soothing to mosquito bites, and irritations of the skin of every nature.

It is advisable, in order to clear the complexion permanently, to cleanse the blood; then the wash would be of advantage.

TO STOP HICCUPS

To stop hiccoughing place the blade of a table knife on the tongue and let it rest for a few minutes.

STYE

Ida Lowell Wilson Baldeschwiler born 1883

When a stye begins to come on the eye, it can be removed by rubbing with a gold ring.

RINGWORM

Crack open a green walnut hull, crush, and apply the juice to the affected area with cotton.

RED BUG BITES

To be used to control red bug bites: Strip child and grease all over with bacon drippings. They will stop itching almost immediately.

SPIDER BITES

A supply of spiderweed was gathered while it was still green and stored in a box to stay soft, if any of the family were bitten by a spider, some of the spiderweed was mixed into a poultice and placed on the bite.

CHIGGERS

An ounce of sulphur rubbed on the skin will keep the chiggers away.

ANT BITE

A solution of vinegar and soda, or a strong solution of salt.

CUTS OR PUNCTURE WOUNDS

Clean wound well and apply a piece of fat bacon or fat back. Tie on or strap on for several days. Change if you need to do so.

LAXATIVE

The pioneer mothers, who also acted as nurses, purged and vomited their patients. In East Texas the "Hog Haw" grew quite abundantly west of the Sabine Valley. The berries of this bush gathered fresh, bruised in water and the liquid strained off, was a pleasant laxative. The dried berries were boiled and the liquid from the decoction was more effective and almost cathartic.

BLADDER AND KIDNEY TROUBLE

Bladder and kidney trouble, probably the result of supermeat diets, were of frequent occurrence among the pioneers. The chief home remedy was "Eupatorium" known as grovel root, which was boiled to make a decoction.

KIDNEY TROUBLE

A quart jar full of watermelon seeds was placed on a shelf in case anyone had trouble with his kidneys. A few of the seeds were boiled in a little water, then the water was drained into a glass or cup and left to settle. A draught of it would stop the trouble.

LIVER REMEDY

After the balmonia had shed its blooms in October, the weeds were gathered. Although bitter tasting, it was thought good for the liver. The weeds were broken into pieces and boiled, drained, and the water strained; enough sugar was added to make a thin syrup to be poured down an ailing child's throat.

SORES

When children had sores that didn't heal fast. The sarsaparilla tea would straighten them out and purify their blood to prevent a "risin" which could be cured by a poultice made from maderia vines.

COLDS AND FEVER

For colds and fever a salve was made of baking soda and lard and placed behind each ear, under each arm and on the bottoms of the feet. This was supposed to run the fever down and broomweed tea to stop the coughing.

FEVERS

The Texas mountain pink was one of the most dependable fever remedies known to the early settlers. The plants were collected while in blossom and dried, then soaked in brandy. The dosage was a tsp. a day.

AGUE, CHILLS AND FEVER

The bark of the red wood or Judas tree was ground and used instead of quinine. Chili peppers were prescribed in heavy doses.

A tea made by steeping a tsp. of the white inside bark of a Mexican persimmon in six cups of water was found to stop the chills.

One cure was to dig a ditch a foot deep, strip off all clothing and bury oneself with the exception of the head in the warm earth. Then sleep there all night and the chills and fever was said not to return.

ASTHMA

Bees honey and sulphur was highly recommended to treat asthma as were buttercups pounded.

One suggested treatment involved a trip to the river to catch a frog. The patient then pries open the frogs mouth, blows his breath into the frog before daylight. Before sundown the frog dies, but the asthma is gone forever.

BIRTHMARKS

A child's birthmark would disappear if rubbed with raw meat, and the meat was buried.

BLEEDING

An artery which had been cut was to be seared with a hot iron.

Another cure was to wear a bunch of keys or a bullet around the neck to stop bleeding.

BUNIONS

Bunions were treated by tying fresh salt pork over the bunion and changing nightly.

RINGWORM

When working with cattle, a person could get ringworm. The remedy was to cut a green walnut in two halves and press half on the parasite.

RHEUMATISM

Sleeping with a pelon dog of Mexican variety (Chihuahua) "cures" the rheumatism, but generally the dog dies.

Another remedy was to rub rattlesnake oil on the affected parts and wear the rattlers around the neck.

Dirt out of a graveyard walked over for ten consecutive nights by the patient was thought to cure rheumatism.

Another remedy was to place a pint of vinegar in an empty whiskey bottle and add a handful of large red ants. To be shaken well and applied internally and externally.

CHAPPED HANDS

One cure for chapped hands was to rub them with buffalo tallow, and then leave them unwashed until they were healed.

COLDS

Colds were treated in various ways; broom weed tea, red pepper tea and horehound tea. Rock candy and horehound boiled together made a fine syrup for colds. Whiskey was frequently used to cure a cold.

DROPSY

One beef gall to a quart of whisky was advised. To be shaken well and drunk three times a day.

BONE FELONS

A ranch remedy for felons was strong lye boiled with tobacco and corn meal to make a poultice.

ARROW WOUNDS

Capt. James Cook relates that he was shot by a Lipan Indian on the Nueces River with a poisoned arrow. The Mexicans in the party burned the spines off a cactus leaf, inserted pepper berries in the wound and bound the cactus to it. Captain Cook recovered.

LOCKJAW

A prominent "cure" for lockjaw was a tea made of cockroaches. Lockjaw was a common ill and was often treated by this tea, according to many old settlers.

GUN SHOT WOUNDS

One of the remedies for gun shot wounds was to keep the wound wet with a rag dipped in cold water. This was the best known remedy in early days.

LUNACY

Lunacy was treated by applying the buttercup plant to the back of the neck during the wane of the moon.

LUNG TROUBLE

Watercress in large quantities was taken by the patient for lung trouble.

PNEUMONIA

Pneumonia was frequently treated with onion poultices.

SKUNK BITES

Skunk bites were treated with salt, or by cauterizing with a hot iron. Skunk bites were frequently fatal.

SORE THROAT

A gargle made from agarita bush roots was found good. Tying your sock around your neck was thought to be effective. The inner bark of a live oak tree boiled made a fine gargle.

TEETHING BABIES

One of the best remedies for a fretful teether was thought to be to give it three large rattles from a snake tied on a red cord and to leave it there until the teeth came in.

FIRST AID OUTFIT

Alcohol—for rubbing pains, strain and sprains and to refresh skin during an illness
Ammonia—2 oz. or ½ tsp. in water for faintness
Boric Acid—1½ tsp. in a glass of hot water to use as eye wash
Carbolated vaseline—treatment of burns
Castor Oil—one to two tbsp. to cleanse a persons inside body
Oil of Cloves—for toothache
Iodine—3½ per cent for wounds
Syrup of Ipecas—1 tsp., followed by warm water to cause vomiting
Bacon fat—tied with cloth to bring out a thorn or splinter
Sulphur—eaten to prevent boils

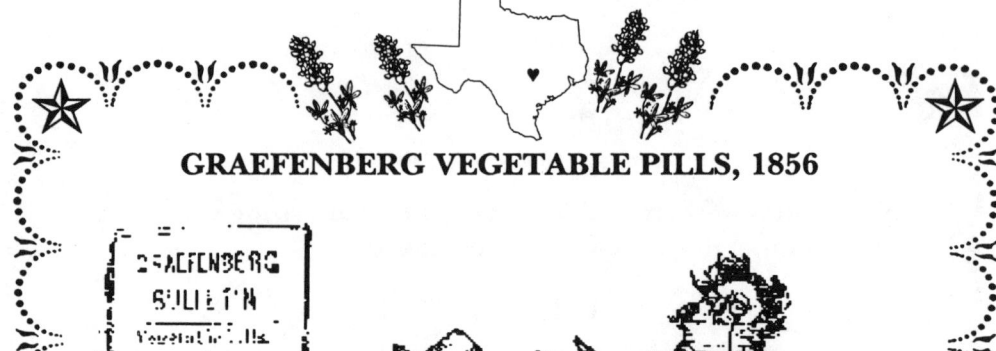

GRAEFENBERG VEGETABLE PILLS, 1856

People flock to the Graefenberg Bulletin for information!

[Copied from *1856, Almanac: Francis T. Dauffau's TEXAS*. Dr. Dauffau purchased the property that was the Republic owned Presidents House property and lived there with his family. Mrs Daffau was a DRT member.]

"The methods usually adopted for the eradication of disease have been justly compared to the celebrated burning of Moscow. The enemy was obliged to retire for want of means to live, but the poor country was so devastated that it required a long time for its restoration. Violent doses of medicine sometimes drive out the disease among the general ruin, but the wreck still remains a source of life-long sorrow. The remedy clearly indicated, is one which will perform its work upon the *disease*, letting alone those portions of the system already well.

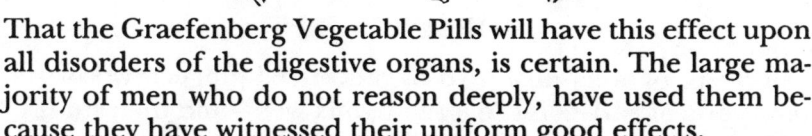

That the Graefenberg Vegetable Pills will have this effect upon all disorders of the digestive organs, is certain. The large majority of men who do not reason deeply, have used them because they have witnessed their uniform good effects.

Cultivated physicians, of liberal views, have examined them carefully, and being convinced from this examination that they ought to be beneficial, have adopted them into their practice, and found them fully equal to their expectations. The only ones who now raise a syllable against them are ignorant physicians whose minds are bounded by a mere name, and who discard everything without examination as soon as they learn that comes outside the precincts of their own sect."

PILE OINTMENT

Take a teacup of hog's lard (more or less) put in a flat tin or peter dish, and take two bars of lead, flattened a little, and rub the lard with the flat ends, and between them till it becomes black or a dark lead color. Then burn equal parts of cavendish tobacco and old shoe leather in an iron vessel till charred; powder these and mix into the lard until it becomes thick ointment. Use once or twice a day as an ointment for the piles.

FOR STIFF JOINTS

Take about half a pint of angleworms (usually known as fishworms), put them in a glass bottle, add one ounce of oil of sassafras and spirits of turpentine, two tbsp. of salt, let stand in the sun two or three days, or till they are dissolved; or if there is not sun, dissolve by gentle heat near the fire. Then strain through flannel to exclude the dirt, and bottle for use. This liniment, freely used twice a day and preserved, will overcome the stiffness of any joint, where it is possible to do so.

DROPSY RECEIPT

Two tbsp. of steel dust, two of pulverized ginger, two of sulphur, one of garusaliur (oat seed), mix well — and then stir it in a pint of honey, put it in a glass jar — so you can stir good with a case knife. Take one bite on the case knife 3 times a day and do not eat any grease while taking it, don't eat anything but bread and coffee or tea. Dose be governed by the bowels, if they move more than twice a day, lessen the dose, if you can't get the steel dust, get an old file and get a blacksmith to melt it — beat it in to dust — sift it through a muslim bag to get the lumps out.

Conversion Charts

CONVERSIONS FROM THEN TO NOW

The old way of measuring ingredients, oven heat, and even size and type of ingredients were substantially different in modern times. These conversions charts will help to convert old recipes to modern usage.

1. Eggs were much smaller than modern-day large eggs. Small eggs should always be used with old recipes.

2. When the recipe says "butter the size of an egg," compare it to a small egg or use about two tbsp. of butter.

3. There was no cake flour and all the baking was done with common flour. Many times cooks mixed corn starch with the flour.

4. There was no refined white sugar. The sugar was more like our light brown sugar.

WEIGHTS AND MEASURES

Ten eggs equal one pound. Of brown sugar: one pound two ounces is one quart; powdered sugar: one pound one ounce is one quart; loaf sugar broken: one pound is one quart. Butter, when soft: one pound is one quart; Indian meal: one pound two ounces is one quart; wheat flour: one pound is one quart.

BAKING

Names given to the various temperature stages for baking:

Slow oven	250 degrees to 325 degrees F.
Moderately slow oven	326 degrees to 349 degrees F.
Moderate oven	350 degrees to 375 degrees F.
Moderately hot oven	376 degrees to 399 degrees F.
Hot oven	400 degrees to 449 degrees F.
Quick oven	450 degrees to 500 degrees F.

TABLES OF WEIGHTS AND MEASURES

1901

60 drops = 1 tsp.
3 tsp. = 1 liquid oz.
2 tbsp. = 1 liquid oz.
4 tbsp. = ¼ cup
16 tbsp. = 1 cup
1 wine glass = ¼ cup
¼ pint = 1 gill
2 cups = 1 pint
2 pints = 1 quart
4 quarts = 1 gallon
8 quarts = 1 bushel
4 pecks = 1 bushel

2 cups granulated sugar = 1 lb.
3½ cups confectioners sugar, sifted = 1 lb.
2¼ cups brown sugar, firmly packed = 1 lb.
2 cups solid meat = 1 lb.
9 medium-sized eggs = 1 lb.
5 whole eggs = 1 cup
8–10 egg whites = 1 cup
13–14 egg yolks = 1 cup
2 cups solid butter = 1 lb.
2 tbsp. butter = 1 oz.
3 cups cornmeal = 1 lb.
4 cups flour = 1 lb.

MEASUREMENTS

1 cup flour = 4 oz.
4 cups flour = 1 lb.
3¼ cups whole wheat flour = 1 lb.
1 tbsp. butter = 1 oz.
1 cup butter = 8 oz.
1 sq. unsweetened chocolate = 1 oz.
1 sq. grated unsweetened chocolate = 5½ tbsp.
1 lb. raisins = 2⅔ cups
1 lb. dates = 2½ cups

3 tsp. = 1 tbsp.
2 tbsp. = 1 fluid oz.
½ cup solid butter = ¼ lb.
1 cup solid butter = ½ lb.
1 cup shelled walnuts = ¼ lb.
1 cup shelled pecans = ⅓ lb.
Juice of 1 lemon = approx. 3 tbsp.
Juice of 1 orange = 5–6 tbsp.
1 tbsp. cornstarch = ½ oz.
1 #1 (8-oz.) can = 1 cup

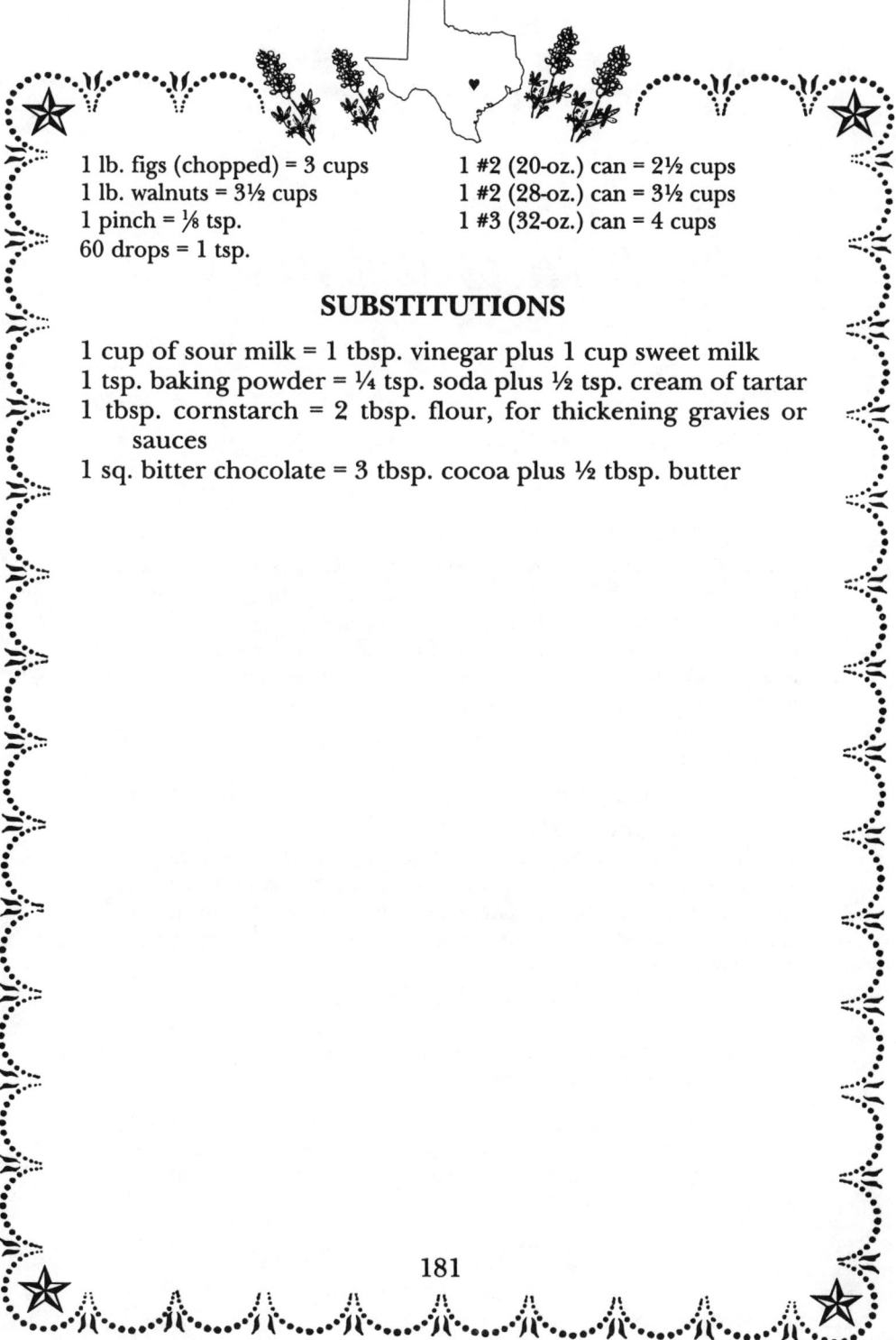

1 lb. figs (chopped) = 3 cups
1 lb. walnuts = 3½ cups
1 pinch = ⅛ tsp.
60 drops = 1 tsp.

1 #2 (20-oz.) can = 2½ cups
1 #2 (28-oz.) can = 3½ cups
1 #3 (32-oz.) can = 4 cups

SUBSTITUTIONS

1 cup of sour milk = 1 tbsp. vinegar plus 1 cup sweet milk
1 tsp. baking powder = ¼ tsp. soda plus ½ tsp. cream of tartar
1 tbsp. cornstarch = 2 tbsp. flour, for thickening gravies or sauces
1 sq. bitter chocolate = 3 tbsp. cocoa plus ½ tbsp. butter

Translations

"Back of the stove" is an expression known to all old-time cooks who used huge black, iron, wood ranges with plenty of space away from the fire box to let things finish cooking slowly and gently. The warming oven of such a stove is ideal for drying mittens, etc., between meals. With double boilers and trivets it is possible to achieve the same slow cooking process on a modern gas or electric stove. The present-day saying "it's cooking on the back burner" must have derived from this custom.

Baking soda is the familiar bicarbonate of soda and was called for in the old recipes either to act as a leavening agent in baking to prevent curdling of milk and tomato dishes, or to provide an aerated texture to such confections as brittle candies. Until the middle 1800s, baking soda was elegantly called "saleratus" and combined with the acidity of buttermilk and sour cream or milk, or such sweeteners as molasses for making quick bread.

Saleratus see baking soda.

Sour milk and cream were natural and staple ingredients in the old kitchen, and buttermilk came directly from the churn.

Spiders were cherished items in the old kitchen. It is nothing more mysterious than a capacious frying pan, preferably of cast iron, in which things fried, simmered or kept warm in a most satisfactory manner.

Contributors

REUBEN HORNSBY CHAPTER
Austin

BARBER, Jean Stafford
BAREFIELD, Joyce Stafford
BROWNING, Julia McLaurin
BYERS, Pauline Rowe
CALLAHAN, Paula Kay Kluge
CALLAN, Myrtle Hornsby
CHRISTIANSON, Joanne Platt
CLARK, Florence Mae Alexander
DITTLINGER, Carol Ann
DOLECEK, Mary Jane Hornsby
DOUGLAS, Willie Lois McCullough
FRANKLIN, Edith Jane Peterson
FRANKLIN, Vivian Leigh
HALL, Nanene Gilbert
HARRIS, Laura Upton
JOHNSON, Sarah Katherine Sneed
KRUMM, Patricia Kay Dittlinger
MANGUM, Florence Irene Landin
MCCALLA, Mary Ailine Gilbert
MCCLOSKEY, Rebecca Hornsby
MEEKS, Cynthia Joe Franklin
MEINARDUS, Lola Ellen Upton
MENGES, Mary Darlene Mangum
PATTERSON, Dixie Marie Hornsby
PEARCE, Lilla Donnan Barnes
PLATT, Thelma Rowe
PRECURE, Claudia Rene Upton
SEPULVADO, Wilna Laurene Sneed
SHEA, Sandra Hiss Barnes
SWITZER, Martha Mary Mellown
UPTON, Betty Jo Walker
WILLIAMS, Nancy Allyn Mangum
WILSON, Mary Jo Upton

STEPHEN F. AUSTIN CHAPTER
Austin

BABCOCK, Beatrice Heller
BAXTER, Rea Buchanan
BIGBEE, Barbara Joan Daniel
BUTLER, Marguerite Walling
CAIN, Julia Ione Biggs
CARTER, Mary Virginia Donaldson
CHANCE, Jennie Marie Dannelley
COHLMIA, Ruth L. Buckalew
DECKER, Helen Elkins
HALL, Helen Reichert
HARDT, Janet Ruth
HATLEY, Danya Carol Cable
HUMPHRY, Ruth Blalock
JOHNSON, Susan Janette Porter
KOEHLER, Ruth Caroline Hardt
KOLB, Debra Lynn Parker
MESSER, Bonnie McWhorter
RAGSDALE, Crystal Sasse
SHEPHERD, Daisy Fulton
TARLTON, Doris Virginia Jane Morral
TREADWELL, Mattie Evelyn
TUCKER, Vashti Louise Smith
WELCH, Sara Patricia Devine
WILLIAMS, Mary Ellen Dannelley
WILSON, Janice Lee Williams

TEXIAN CHAPTER
Austin

ANGUS, Hazel Houston
CHAPIN, Judith Morehead
CLOUD, Patricia Ann Eppright
CRAFT, Vaughn Dane
DALRYMPLE, Mildred Banford Inks
FELL, Anna Pearle Secrest
FLOW, Carol June Green
FLYNN, Margaret Elizabeth Caldwell
FRANKE, Gethrel Arlon
GARRETT, Sandra Dawn Polley
GHOLSON, Lillian Rachel Magill
GOWEN, Mary Carrington
GRIFFIN, Patricia Lel
HAWKINS. Martha Lel Purcell
HENDERSON, Mary Agnes Connelly
JORDON, Billie Bernice Connell
LOONEY, Rowena T. Darter
MANDAVILLE, Thelma Brandon
MARTIN, Betty Mae Raven
MIDDLETON, Nancy Newborn
MOREHEAD, Judith English
MORGAN, Elizabeth Anne Deal
POLLARD, Ann Durling
POLLEY, Cynthia Louise
POLLEY, Louise Green
POWER, Beulah Williams
PURCELL, Margaret Beatrice Howze
ROGERS, Elizabeth Stoneham
RICHARDSON, Nena Newborn
ROGERS, Elizabeth Stoneham
SCHWARTZ, Catherine Elizabeth Hall
SMITH, Cynthia Marie
SMITH, Dorothy Marie Davis
SPALDING, Diana Lynn Fuste
SPENCER, Patsy Lee Gunn
TWEEDY, Karen Lee Green
WALKER, Cheryl Diane Polley
WEISS, Helen Kay Tyler
WESTBROOK, Carlene Lee
WRIGHT, Hazel Elizabeth Henderson

WILLIAM BARRET TRAVIS CHAPTER
Austin

ADRIAN, Lucile Winters
ALTMAN, Helen Alsup
ARNETT, Cleo Mae
ARNOLD, Kenzie Lou Box
BAGGETT, Jewell Maurine Spark
BARKER, Cathy Gayle Mumford
BARRON, Phyllis McAnelly
BASS, Caroline Boales
BENNETT, Gloria Joyce Walton
BERWICK, Eloise Allene Munlin
BLOEBAUM, Ray Pearl Holder
BOWERS, Julie Lee Gibson
BRANNEN, Jennie Alva Morrow
BREES, Amy Hightower
BROGREN, Eleanor Halton
BROWN, Lillian Baggett
BUGG, Mildred Alice Webb
BULLARD, Karen Leigh Thompson
BULLOCK, Gloria Jan Felts
CADWALLADER, Margaret Erie Leslie
CARLSON, Margaret L. Rader
CARMICHAEL, Margaret Stiles Farrar
CASTILLE, Lillian Virginia Sibley
CAWLFIELD, Lucy Holland
CHIODO, Gloria Ann Friedman
CHOTE, Rosa Catherine Woolsey
CLAPHAM, Rosemary Curry
COLEMAN, Ommie Ruth Barton
CONNER, Belva Irene Lee
COOK, Eula Belle Maley
COOKE, Sarah W. Parmele
COOLEY, Carolyn Lindley
COOLEY, Julia Loyce Haynie
COSTLEY, Maria Celeste
COUSER, Mildred Arbuckle
COX, Patricia Ann Legan
CRAIN, Mary Genevieve
CUNNINGHAM, Cherry Eileen Larson
CUNNINGHAM, Laura Catherine Voss
DANIEL, Jean Houston Baldwin
DAUGHERTY, Carolyn Ann Root
DEBARBRIE, Margaret Anne Brown
DELANEY, Virginia Nell Rader
DILLON, Denise Lorraine Stuckey
DOLHOF, Mary Katherine Decherd
DULAN, Bess Gunn
EAST, Dawn Carolene
EGG, Frances Geraldine Duncan
ELLISON, Melva Kirchhof
FEDOR, Rosalie Ann
FERRALL, Mary Virginia Root
FEUERBACHER, Marie Dolores Behr
FLEISCHER, Mary Beth
FORISTER, M. C.
FRENCH, Sylvia Dee Woodson
GAGE, Carol Boatman
GERSTENBERG, Mary Virginia Lemburg
GIBLIN, Ura Maye Rogers
GIBSON, Dorothy Mae Franklin
GILMER, Elizabeth Lynne
GILMER, Rebecca Sue Stockton
GLOBER, Catharine Barry Crain
GOINES, Ruth Lentsch
GOUDREAU, Barbara Jane Langham
GREEN, Katherine Ann Gerstenberg
GREEN, Moya Jan Wilkinson
GUNN, Charlotte Ruth Hill
HANKEY, Joy Wilson
HARDIN, Adena Elizabeth Ward

HARDIN, Sharon Ann
HAYES, Donna Katherine Loyless
HIGHTOWER, Colleen Ward
HOLLIS, Opal Klutts
HUTH, Inez Carmen Schilling
IGO, June Kathryn Jones
IZZO, Dianne Louise Schoener
JACKSON, Una Evelyn Woods
JOHNSON, Bertie Louise Franklin
JOHNSON, Carol Jean McAnelly
JOHNSON-NALTY, Pamela Susan
KELLEY, Suzanne Arnold
KNOX, Loretta Virginia Conn
KOONTZ, Patsy Quinn Wilkinson
LANGSTON, Dale Lynn Holtzclaw
LARSON, Zilla LaVerne Luce
LAWHON, Mabel Cobb Evard
LAWHON, Mary Ethel Huth
LAWHON, Sara Dyann
LESHIKAR, Nancy Lee Burrell
LOCK, Dr Robin Anne Hartman
LONG, Ellen Clare Todd
LUNDELIUS, Hazel Halton
MAGNESS, Mary Josephine Smith
MALLESKE, Glynda Jean Walton
MARCELLUS, Lola Leona Boales
MATTHEWS, Myreta Julia
MCANELLY, Betty Jean McCarty
MCCORMICK, Sandra Kay Coleman
MCCUTCHEON, Ethel Johnson
MCGINTY, Patricia Ann Bennett
MCMASTERS, Daisye Maxine Sibley
MECREDY, Virginia Ann Taylor
MECREDY, Virginia Ann
MILLER, Bessie Louise Hendrick
MILLER, Katherine Lentz
MORGAN, Jeanell Campbell
MUNDS, Helen Colleen
MURRAY, Virginia Louise Castille
NEATHERY, Faye Wilson
NIEBUHR, Althea Newsome
NULTY, Lois Smith

ORR, Rebecca Ann Moore
PARKINGTON, Margaret Underwood
PATTERSON, Myrtle Lorena Schuchardt
PEREZ, Ann Katherine Lemburg
PERRINE, Ione Anne Pittman
PETERSON, Sylvia Faye Rost
PETERSON, Tyra Kay Fedor
PIERCE, Margaret Helen Ryals
PLACKE, Mary Sue Pace
POE, Ila Mae
POLK, Bonnie Gibson
PORTER, Betty Harrelson
PREECE, Henrietta Lucille Rader
PRESTON, Edna Retta Rutherford
PURDY, Catherine Colleen Bruce
RABB, Lillian Bell
RADE, June Elizabeth Thorp
RAEKE, Jane Reiplinger
RATHBONE, Bettye Jean Schmidt
REDWINE, Darryle Jane Price
REEVES, Bonnie Faye Mills
REININGER, Evelyn Genevieve Pehl
RICHARDSON, Mary Jo Dulaney
RICKERT, Mary Therese
RICKERT, Mary Theresa Burleson
ROBLES, Laura Ann Gilmer
ROST, Vera Lerleen Wilson
ROUTH, Fay Campbell
RYALS, Caroline Davis Roberts
SANDLIN, Anne Marie Rountree
SARYTCHOFF, Sheryl Hankey
SCHORR, Hattie Norene Gorbet
SEALS, Ellen Lorraine Short
SEAVER, Sydney Dawn Holleman
SELLARS, Claytie Louise Jenkins
SHAFER, Elva Jean Lankford
SHIVERS, Shari Lynn Oualline
SIMMONS, Albertine Elizabeth Holcomb
SIMMONS, Virginia Kathleen Laswell
SINGLETON, Mary Virginia Haynie
SMILAND, Marilyn Carroll
SMITH, Emma Grace Gilliland

SMITH, Linda Kay Boatman
SMITH, Posey Baggett
SPONBERG, Ruby Anzie Ponton
STANSBURY, Martha Faulk
STONE, Dona Locke
STRAITON, Elizabeth Yeiser
STUCKEY, Mary Ann Dillard
SUTTLE, Alison Hightower
TAYLOR, Mary Ellen Martin
TAYLOR, Sue Saul
THOMPSON, Montie Ray West
THORNBURG, Ann Hightower
TOMHAVE, Jetty Ann McDonald
TOMHAVE, Joy Christine
TONEY, Demp
TUTTLE, Josephine Estelle Ulit
UNDERWOOD, Frances Brady
WALKER, Virginia Sansom
WARBURTON, Zellane Jeanelle Golden
WATSON, Eunice Mae Dobie
WEST, Martha Mae Wilson
WETTIG, Sandra Gail Thompson
WHITE, Clarice Elaine Ellison
WILKINSON, Nelma Arlene Toney
WILLIAMS, Betty Bell Smith
WILLIAMS, Christie Virginia Stanberry
WILLIAMS, Mildred Shirley Fleischer
YANCY, Frances Virginia Howell
ZUCKNICK, Trona Wilson

BARON DE BASTROP CHAPTER

Bastrop

BARBER. Shirley Irene Prewitt
BIRDWELL, Gladys Lee Bryant
BRYANT, Mary Ann Ramsey
BRYANT, Ruth Ann
CHAPMAN, Constance Marie Mattord
CLAMPIT, Pamelia Alyce Roubison
FERGUSON, Alyce Annette Boscamp
GODWIN, Frances Maurine Perkins
JOHNSON, Valerie Kaye Kite
MAJORS, Johnnie JoNell Hancock
MAULDIN, Mary Eunice Robbins
MAULDIN, Patricia Elaine Roubison
MCWHORTER, Agnes Margaret MaAnaney
MEUTH, Gladys Hardy
ROBINSON, Mary Gail
ROUBISON, Kim Elizabeth
SANDERS, Robbie Dean Moore
SHARP, Effie Augustus Davis
SMITH, Ruth Eleanor
VALENTA, Marilyn Kay Majors
WOLF, Evelyn Frances Farris

DR. WILHELM KEIDEL CHAPTER
Fredericksburg

BALZEN, Helen Ann
BALZEN, Jarline Annie
BELL, Susan Gail Spradley
BERTRAND, Betty Lou Balzen
BINGHAM, Sheila Gail Hohmann
BROWN, Susan Lee Ethel
CADE, Barbara Ann Donalson
CARTER, Grace Irene Boles
COON, Nancy Ann Reams
COX, Peggy Joan Nixon
CRENWELGE, Cheryl Ann
CRENWELGE, Katherine Evelyn Schlentz
CRENWELGE, Leah Renee
DAIGLE, Mary Kay Clark
ETHEL, Betty McElroy
FRANCIS, Evelyn Ruth Milberger
GOLD, Viola May Schmidt
HAGMANN, Nancy Jan Roberts
HALEY, Jane Spradley
HANNUM, Helen Dorothy Kothe
HARRIS, Dennis Heinen
HAYWARD, Nancy Ann Schlentz
HEINEN, Barbara Claire Schmidt
HEINEN, Donna Jane
HOGUE, Mary Kathryn Jones
HUGHES, Penny Perry
JONES, Katheryn Roberts
KUNZ, Deanne Heinen
MARSCHALL, Betty Jeanette Rogers
MCCARTHY, Janice Spradley
MENDEZ, Nina Louise Nixon
METZGER, Leta Ann Thaxton
OEHLER, Esther Minna Schmidt
PERRY, Victoria Keidel
SCHLENTZ, Mildred Evelyn Besch
SCHMIDT, Emily Keidel
SCHOESSOW, Cristol Forres Nixon
SCHWARZ, Edna Yuvonne Behrns
STEGALL, Carolyn Helen Hogue
STEVENSON, Harriet Leigh Hogue
URBANEC, Kelley Renee
URBANEC, Linda Sue Nixon

GONZALES CHAPTER

Gonzales

AVERY, Joy Green
BARFIELD, Louise Mitchell
BOOTHE, Florence Dubose
BUFFUM, Elizabeth Jane Froehner
CHENAULT, Carey Fleda Hoskins
COLLINS, Audrey Bright
CROZIER, Laura Bright
DENMAN, Ruth Kokernot
DILWORTH, Hercel Lucille Orts
EHRIG, Kathleen Moore
ESKA, Elizabeth Anne
ESKA, Patricia Lee Taylor
FINK, Elizabeth Hortense Houston
FLOYD, Raguet Hoskins
FOWLKES, Deborah Stulting
FRIEDRICH, Marilyn Kay Walker
GINDLER, Marian Blanche Meinert
GLOVER, Ola Kellogg
GREGG, Maud Kelley
GUSTAFSON, Margaret Griffith
HAMILTON, Odelle
HINES, Lee Ann Nagel
ILEY, Jayne Ellen Nagel
JAHNKE, Mary Beauford
JOHNSON, Carol Ann Richardson
KILLION, Martha Ann Baker
KOKERNOT, Mabel Joy
KOKERNOT, Rosemary Kibbe Breeden
KREUTZER, Rachel Virginia Kelley
LEWIS, Eva Coe
MAULDIN, Sandra Lynn Fink
MCDOUGAL, Beulah M. Bennet
MILLS, Melanie Moore
MOORE, Mary Elizabeth Hindman
NAGEL, Mildred Annette Shuler
NOWOTNY, Wilma Holzmann
POPE, Mary Louise Barfield
RAYES, Margaret Lewis
RICHARDSON, Jo Ann Nowotny
RICHARDSON, Zelma Jane Tyree
SCOTT, Margaret Shearn
SHANKLIN, Mary Cleveland
SMITH, Harriet Beatrice Dikes
SMITH, Ruth Janet Lauren
STULTING, Tommie Voitle
THORN, Lottie Robinson
VACKAR, Edna Askey
VOLLENTINE, Genevieve Bradley
WALKER, Faye Bennet
WATERS, Rosemary Bennet

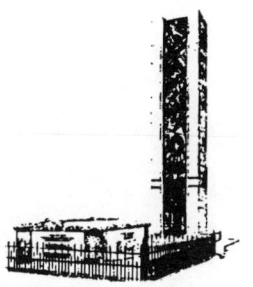

MONUMENT HILL CHAPTER
La Grange

ALBRECHT, Dorothy Mae Wallace
BALDWIN, Kathleen Stuesser
BEAN, Elizabeth Belle Fietsam
BEHLEN, Deborah Ann Fietsam
CHAPMAN, Joan Marie Phillips
COWAN, Julia Stuesser Anderson
DARNELL, Ruby Ann Matthews
DIETZEL, Sadie Florine Wallace
DYER, Lillian LeNora Stuermer
FIETSAM, Diana Lynn
FISCHER, Kathryn Barkley
GARBUS, Cynthia Eileen Karnau
GUETHLE, Martha Susan Moss
HIGGINS, Deborah Delaine Belk
HILL, Betty Jean Phillips
HOFFMAN, Doris Ida Bean
JACKSON, Mary Elizabeth Oldfield
JERVIS, Lillian Christine Dyer
JOHNSON, Rox Ann Albrecht
KARNAU, Eileen Louise Frank
KARNAU, Sally Ann
KEILERS, Dawn
KEILERS, Elva Ann Meiners
KOCUREK, Grace Amy Matthews
LUTHER, Bridget Bean Schultz
MABRY, Sarah Anne Peel
MARBLE, Ida Carolyn Calvin
MCLAIN, Jana Kay Fischer
MEINERS, Beatrice Marie Hagemann
MILLER, Marilyn Ann Frank
ROGERS, Glenn Denise Higgins
STANCIK, Darlene Marie
STANCIK, Joyce Marie Matthews
STUESSER, Lillian Fietsam
WENSKE, Deena Delaine Higgins
WILLIAMS, Imogene Fietsam Baker

ORAN MILO ROBERTS CHAPTER
Lampasas

CARPENTER, Glynda Carson
CASBEER, Carrie Frances
CASBEER, Martha Ann Tumlinson
DANIELL, Mary Ann Easters
DAVIS, Amy Lee
DAVIS, Diane Lynn
DAVIS, Lillian Carol Moore
DAVIS, Margaret June Moore
EASTERS, Carol Sue
FRITZ, Peggy Elloise Smith
GOEN, Suzanne Smith
GOODSON, Lila Hall
HANER, Rebecca Patteson
HEMPHILL, Alice Elizabeth Berry
HURST, Leona Ann Hunter
KEELE, Suzanne Curtis
KORN, Susan Elaine Webb
LAURENCE, Denise Lorraine Davis
MACHMEIER, Judith Annette Hall
MCCARVILLE, Cindy Davis
MILLER. Molly Neal Patteson
MOORE, Mary Thelma Fritz
MULLINS, Betty Morene Perry
MULLINS, Tammy Louise
MULLINS, Wilda Louise Queen
MULLINS, Wrenda Morene
NASH, Charlene Zavalla Eckert
NORCROSS, Virqinia Elizabeth Nash
PATTESON, Ruth Neal Corder
PERSKY, Janice Lynn Berry
POTTS, Janie Sue Glimp
QUEEN, Ola Owdia Ming
RUSH, Alice Elizabeth Langford
SHERBERT, Georganna Patteson
SIMS, Janice Moore
SMITH, Evelyn Moore
SMITH, Sharon
VINEYARD, Sydna Montgomery
WRIGHT, Cynthia Mary
WRIGHT, Mary Carol Northington

LLANO CHAPTER
Llano

BISHOP, Kathy Denise Christopher
BONNET, Betty Earline Elliott
BRADLEY, Aline Estelle Wunneburger
CHRISTIAN, Evelyn Lucille Wheeler
CHRISTOPHER, Geraldine Marie Merkel
COFFMAN, Claudean Ford
CORNELIUS, Mona Lynn Denham
DALTWAS, Sylvista Gean Alexander
DANIEL, Angela Ruth Jordan
DAVENPORT, Frankie Dodson
DYSERT, Gene Harrell
ELLIOTT, Mildred Alline Halliburton
FAIRBURN, Gladys Anna Fritze
FOWLER, Lella Lillian Smith
FOWLER, Marjorie Emma Ahrlett
GAREY, Camille Ann Blackmore
GUTHERY, Janet Sue Bertram
HAHN, Geneva Easter Merkel
HALE, Frances Maxine McCormick
HALLMARK, Flora Maxine Pyle
HANSON, Georgie Elaine Dillingham
HARRIS, Josiephene Elouise Robbins
HOLDER, Helen Jane Carter
JACKSON, Bernice Muriel Barnett
JOHNSON, Norma Elizabeth Pyle
KLEEN, Betty Jo Houck
MACEK, Ruby Joy Ahrlett
MCBRIDE, Joan Zumwalt
MCMULLEN, Billie Marie Merkel
MEINE, Vina Mae Tumlinson
MICHEL, Joy Ruth Dillingham
MILLER, Carmen Mildred Hardt
MILLER, Lydia Anne
MOORE, Bobbie Jean Alexander
MOORE, Eloise Camille Dickinson
OATMAN, Nancy Diane Menefee
OSBOURN, Kathy Elaine Elliott
RANGELEY, Lynda Louise McKinney
RIVES, Jane Sharon Reding
ROBERTSON, Christine Hope Tinney
SHROUT, Dorthell McKinney
SMITH, Nelwyn Ramona
SMITH, Patsy Jane
SMITH, Shirley Gray Blackmore
SPALDING, Sandra Jean Anderson
SWARTZWELDER, Juanita Dahl
TERRY, Helen Leona Draper
THAMES, Betty Sue Ahrlett
THURMOND, Carolyn Joan Garner
TOMBS, Peggy Carolyn Blackmore
VAN HORN, Jane Elizabeth Ray
WADE, Evelyn Christine Smith
WILSON, Imogene
WILSON, Joan
WOODS, Leslie Lynn
WOODS, Linda Sue Bradley
WOOLSEY, Frances Elnora Frazier

CORNELIUS SMITH CHAPTER
Luling

BAKER, Lennie Mae White
BARABAS, Kim Rae Jones
BELL, Debra Lynn Wells
BLACKSTONE, Ms Sandra Deanne Cain
BOLLES, MaryLee Williamson
BOYD, Barbara Lee Tate
BURCH, Ethel Jewel Morgan
BURROWS, Darla Gail Wells
CADDELL, Billie Jo Weeks
CAIN, Dorothy Nell Ivey
CARRIGAN, Esther Lee Beard
CHANCE, Earlayne Summerrow
CHESLEY, Roberta Cook
CLAYTON, Sharon Dianne Cain
CLIFTON, Marcia Barker
COLWELL, Georgia Neoma Edwards
COOK, Mariella Weston
CRAVEN, Janell Colwell
CRISLER, Patricia Louise Fogle
CROWELL, Ople Liddie Colwell
DAMON, Carolyn Sue Carrigan
FRAZIER, Alice Abigail McGaffey
GIBSON Julia Mae Milford
GILKEY, Dorothy Nell Edwards
GROSS, Terri Lee Canter
HALLIBURTON. Linda Kay Hurt
HENDERSHOT, Patsy Evelyn Jones
HENDERSON, Iantha Maxine Moses
HOWELL, Julie Kate Crockett
HUGHES, Nancy Carole Frazier
KOLLERT, Lillie Johanna Eiband
LEET, Carolyn Lee McCulloch
LIGHTSEY, Donna Gayle
LIGHTSEY, Judith Kay Millican
LIGHTSEY, Leslie Carol Gibson
LORENZ, Letha Mae Linscomb
MANNING, Mary Elizabeth McGaffey
MARTIN, Denise Kay Caddell
MCNABB, Peggy Lee Colwell
MIKES, Elizabeth Ann Truesdale
MILFORD, Esther Omega Risinger
MILLER, Cynthia Ann Caddell
MILLICAN, Cindy Lou Bird
MILLICAN, Gertrude Lucille Linscom
MUELLER, Ruby Lee Linscomb
MULLINNIX, Sarah Junell Walker
PATTON, Patsy Dee Canter
PHILLEY, Corinne Marie Peirce
PITTMAN, Darla Jean Davis
RIHN, Carolyn Yvonne Gilkey
ROBBINS, Shelia Kay Truesdell
SAUNDERS, Linda Lanay Frazier
SMITH, Cheryl Lyn
SMITH, Rev. Linda Margaret Watkins
SMITH, Mary Ann Haygood
TRUESDELL, Cordella Ruth McNabb
TURNER, Eunice Muriel Smith
VOTAW, Dorothy Jean White
WESTBROOK, Madeline Maxine Watkins
WHITE, Andra Pierson
WHITLEY, Marjorie Ann Collins
WHITLEY, Susan Elaine
WILKERS0N, Betsy Ellen Gilkey
WOOD, Peggy Irma Paine
WOOLLEY, Cynthia Denise White

Home of Ferdinand Lindheimer
1801~1879

FERDINAND LINDHEIMER CHAPTER

New Braunfels

ACKER. Nora Victoria Sides
ADAMS, Diane-Caprice Felger
ANDERSON, Mary Ann Hanz
BAERTL, Marcia Jan Burkhardt
BARKER, Sudie Ellen Wray
BATCHELOR, Martha Lou Barker
BERKOWITZ, Candy Jeanne Felger
BOOTHE, Ruby Marie Lindsey
BUBLIK. Wanda Sue McDougall
BURRUS, Dorcas Ann Cunningham
BYRD, Lynne Marie Offerman
CALLAHAN, Carole Elizabeth Leissner
CAMPBELL, Dorothy Ann Gerhardt
CARAWAY, Frankie Elaine Smith
CARROLL, Anne Catherine Rousseau
CLARK, Dallas Dorothy Arnold
COLDEWAY, Eleanor Marie Kneupper
COLLINS, Georgia Ann Garner
COUNCIL, Vicki Anne Felger
CUMING, Valerie Susan Felger
DAVIS, Betty Sue Walker
DAVIS, Betty Jeanne Harvell
DEASY, Kimberly Ann Grimm
DEDEN, Eleanor Elizabeth Cosby
DIETERT, Linda Kay Pfannstiel
DOVE, Barbara Jo Coleman
DUHON, Mildred Bernice Allen
EDISON, Amy Cynthia Reeves
EVANS, Geraldine Hicks
FELGER, Jeanette E. Streuer
FOLEY, Alice Adelphia King
FOLEY, Ramona Yvonne
GARRETT, Susie Lorene Smith
GERHARDT, Esther Karbach Raby
GRAMS, Lois Jean Smith
GREENE, Christina Tristram Engelhardt
GREER, Ella Jean Mitchell
GRIMM, Agnes Louise Glasscock
GRIMM, Mary Ann Moore
GUENZEL, Delitha Lou Acker
HAIN, Cynthia Jo Felger
HARDIN, Mary Elizabeth Beecroft
HENDERSON, Iris Lynn Mangum
HENLEY, Linda Sue Reeves
HOCKER, Emily Alice Burkhart
HOLM, Marie Louise Shelly
HORNE, Mary Elizabeth Barker
HOWARD, Mattie Cordelia Nelson

HUDSON, Miriam Ann
HUDSON, Verna Alice Allen
JACKSON, Geneva Joann Smith
JACKSON, Patricia Carol Timberlake
JACOB, Denise Hall
JOLES, Paula Lynn Foley
JORDAN, Linda Sharyl Bond
KIMPLE, Sheila Rae Evans
KLEMMEDSON, Carolyn Maurine Lozo
KNOWLES, Frances Elizabeth Hovestadt
KNOX, Alison Patricia
KNOX, Ashley Joan
KNOX, Tracy Rachele
LANGFORD, Mary Ellis Burrus
LARSON, Cynthia Diane Mayer
LEISSNER, Carole Margaret Karbach
LOINES, Patricia Joann Jackson
LONG, Linda Jean Holm
LOVE, Gladys Marie Walker
LOZO, Mary Elizabeth Williams
MAGEL, Isabel Leone
MALMSTEAD, Antonette Louise Bolton
MARTIN, Ann Jeannine Foley
MITCHELL, Lucy Marie Betts
MITCHELL, Verily Beatrice Reeves
MOORE, Joyce Jeane Avery
MORRIS, Jeannette Marie Mueller
MOUDY, Elizabeth Emma Allen
MULHERN, Claudine Wilson
MURDOCK, Mary Ellen Guenzel
OFFERMAN, Ida Marie Streuer

PAULGER, Kelly Renee Knox
PEARCE, LaVerne Schwab
PEARCE, Nancy Jean
POE, Karen Lynette Garrett
PROUD, Lesley Cecilla
PROUD, Luciclaire Rankin
RASOR, Patricia Isabelle Anderson
REEVES, Billye Jo
ROGERS, Emily Ruth Barker
SCHMIDT, Amy Caroline
SCHMIDT, Carolyn May Grimm
SCHMIDT, Sarah Leonda Williams
SCHOCH, Mary Jane Kincaid
SCHWAB, Valeska Edna Pfannstiel
SMISSAERT, Isabelle Arnold
SMISSAERT, Laura Isabelle
SMITH, Margaret May Lassig
SMITH, Wanda
SPAIN, Bette Lu Offerman
SPENCER, Iva-Lee Neese
STEVENS, Cynthia Anne Holm
STEVENSON, Mabel Olifia Metzger
STOVALL, Brenda Louise Malmstead
TALAAT, Martha Amanda Burrus
TIELKE, Linda Sue Hovestadt
VOGES, Beverlyn Darleen Altwein
WARE, Barbara Elaine Mitchell
WILLIAMS, Elsie Virginia Willis
WOODS, Mary Gayle Pearce
YOEHLE, Florine Vickery

MARTIN WELLS CHAPTER
Round Rock

ASTON, Mary Bettye Clampitt
BABCOCK, Janie Thompson
BALL, Margaret Maxine Duncan
BENTON, Myrle Dee Grubbs
BEVERIDGE, Tammye Thompson
BROOKS, E. Bunnie Louise Bunn
BRYSON, Rachel Estelle Asher
BUNNER, Sue Ann Bundick
CANIZALES, Nancy Carolyn McDaniel
CLAMPITT, Mary Bettye Clampett
COOK, Jo Ann Riley
CRADDOCK, Mary Lucille Smith
CURLEY, Ruth Teresa Jenkins
DANNELLEY, Beulah Lois Hoffman
DIGGS, Nettie May Ryals
DISKIN, Margaret Joann Nettles
EICHLER, Florence Schmidt
EUSTACE, Barbara Jean Denny
EUSTACE, Laura Jean
FIELDER, Emabel Baker
FLYNN, Betty Jo Edwards
FORESTER, Willie Ruth Asher
FRIX, Wanda Faye Wilhelm
FULLER, Barbara Gail James
GAINES, Patricia J. Edmundson
GARDNER, Nina Katherine Reavis
GOODSON, Sylvia Frances Mitchell
GOULDING, Jean LaVerne Moss
GOULDING, Peggy Marie
GROSE, Dr. Mary Louise Gore
HARDY, Thelma Lois Schmidt
HARLAN, Karen Luvinia Turner
HARRIS, Ruby June Murray
HAWKINS, Jacquelyn Lee
HENRY, Jo Carol Johnson
HOFFMAN, Virginia Dee Atkinson
IMKEN, Frankie Faye Hurt
JOHNSON, Helen Francis Murray
KELLY, Kathryn Anne
KELLY, Nancy Carol Devlin
KETNER, Nancy Hudson
KIRK, Sherry Jean
LOVE, Julie McKean
LOVE, Margaret Janelle McKean
MADDOX, Eleanor Anne Steger
MCALLISTER, Rachel Ann Bryson
MCCLUNG, Monica Lee McIntosh
MCNABB, Jeanne Marie White
MELDE, Betty Lou Murray
MOORE, Kathleen Jeanette Harris
MYERS, Margaret Ruth Harmon
NEVES, Phyllis Louise Tuma
PRICE, Billie Lou Bryson
ROBERTSON, Michelle
SHANKLIN, Judith Stokes
SIMMONS, Janelle Margaret Love
STALLINGS, Dorothy Margaret
STALLINGS, Willie D. Westmoreland
STUCKY, Dlxie Dee Benton
SUTTON, Nadine Ferrell
THOMAS, Lora Lucille Baring
THOMPSON, Frances Elizabeth Mason
THOMPSON, Karen Ruth Dannelly
THOMPSON, Katherine Ruth
TOMLINSON, Anna Reavis
VARAN, Frances Irene Ferrell
VOGT, Rebecca Harris
WHITE, Vesta Cochran
WOODWARD, Frances Cockrell
ZIMMERMAN, Willa June Smith

MOON MCGEHEE CHAPTER
San Marcos

BURTON, Carrie McKinney
DELLA CORTE, Sarah Alice Jones
DENNY, Mary Jane Rehm
DETTMAN, Roberta Meneley
DICKEY, Madaline Constance Russell
DODINGTON, Florence Eleanor Owens
HARRISON, Julie Anna Johnson
JOHNSON, Alice Catherine Word
KASSAW, Carla May Schmidt
MORROW, Alene York
PARMAN, Carolyn Clairice Harman
PARR, Clara Reed Brantley
PERRIN, Andra Jane Parman
PHILLIPS, Virginia Oldham Brock
PINGREY, Betty Jane Dean
SPENCER, Bobbi Jayne Sweeney
TIDWELL, Marilyn Jean Brantley
WALLING, Maude Louise Maddox
WIEGAND, Josephine Spence
WILLIAMSON, Virgie Knutson
WINDLE, Janice King Woods
WOODS, Virginia King Bergfeld

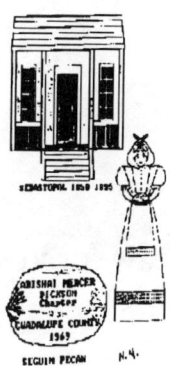

ABISHAI MERCER DICKSON CHAPTER
Seguin

ANDERSON, Doris Louise Ferguson
ARMSTRONG, Mary Avis Boales
BATEY, Olivia Christine Rather
BEHNE, Merle Ruth Moehrig
BENSON, Lelia Florine Palmero
BORMANN, Cindy Ann
BRANDENBERGER, Marjorie S. Blumberg
BRUNS, Florence Julia Wilson
CAMPBELL. Audra Bullard
CRIXELL, Mary Joyce Timmerman
DARILEK, Lucille Koepsel
DRUMM, Laura Belle Shinn
FARR, Wanda Catherine Gustafson
GIDEON, Jodie Suggs
HALM, Annie Maxine Bergfeld
HUBER, Velma Alves
HURT, Katherine Lay Reid
JOHNSON, Judith Marie MyCue
KISER, Kathryn Fay Nagel
KOLB, Helen Marie Tiemann
LOWTHER, Sandra Sue Morris
MYCUE, Arline Henrietta Koepsel
NAGEL, Elsie Koehler
NAUMANN, Nora Ellen Wheeler
ORR, Mary Louise Bergfeld
REED, Carolyn Skidmore
RIVES, June Koepsel
RONSHAUSEN, Edna Mae Lakey
SCHROEDER, Victoria L. Wishkaemper
SCRUTCHIN, Helen Bodemann
SPAHN, Doris Lakey
SPEER, Louie Belle Barrett
TERRY, Mildred Traeger
TRAEGER, Margaret Helen Kolb
TRAEGER, Olivia Schaper
TRAMMELL, Annalyn Christine Koehler
VICKERS, Dora
WHITLEY, Bette Raenelle Powell
ZIELINSKI, LaDelle Piwonka Hebel

ELIZABETH ZUMWALT KENT CHAPTER
Smiley

AVANT, Georgina Bradley Farmer
BANDY, Carla Jo Avant
BRISTER, Annie Lee Burnett
BURNETT, Debra Jean
BURNETT, Virginia Ann Bundick
COLLIER, Beth Anne Loomis
DONALDSON, Maudie Eliz.Whiddon
EMBREY, Cheryl Ann Kuykendall
FREEMAN, Jo Ann Wright
GOROG, Amanda Ruth Anderson
GRAY, Dorothy Geane McRay
GRAY, Kathy Nora Robinson
HAIL, Dr. Francina K.
HALL, Tana James
HASSELL, Melva Ruth Robinson
JACOBS, Melissa Dianne Griffin
JAMES, Cinda-Lin
JAMES, Mareva Glenn
JONAS, Donna Sue Burnett
JORDAN, Sandra Louise Montgomery
KUYKENDALL, Patsy Ruth Tondre
LOESSIN, Edyth Suzanne Tomlinson
LOOMIS, Patricia Gloor Burnett
PARKER, Pearl LaRue Griffin
PARSONS, Marjorie Lee Burnett
PATTESON, Nelda Jean
POOL, Frances Kay Munselle
POPE, Robbie Hyatt
THIGPEN, Connie Lynn
WALKER, Betty Jo
WILLIAMS, Robin Lynn Robinson

Bibliography
(Partial)

Buckeye Cookery and Practical Housekeeping. Buckeye Publishing Company, 1877.
Cooking Recipes of the Pioneers. Bandera, Texas: Frontier Times Museum, 1948.
Davis, L. "Prescriptions and Remedies of the Old Southwest." *Southern Pharmaceutical Journal* 1931 (November 28, 1896).
Dr. Chase's Recipes or Information for Everybody. 1900.
"Elizabeth Johnston Diary." Mrs. Mason Barret Collection of Albert Sidney and Wm. Preston Johnston Papers. New Orleans, Louisiana: Tulane University.
Every Woman Her Own Cook. (Book very old and title page missing), n.d.
Frontier Times. Spring 1962.
Galveston Daily News. 1923.
"Gratuitous to the Patrons of the Graefenberg Company" (patent medicines). *Dr. Francis T. Daffau's Texas Almanac,* 1856.
Jones, Mrs. N. "A Collection of Data Pertaining to Cooking, Early Day Recipes." November, 1946.
Mary Randolph Cookbook. Virginia, ca. 1826.
Numerous recipes contributed by individual members of DRT.
Skoog, Herb C., Bobbie Purdum, and Marie Offerman, eds. Marie Offerman, comp. 1990. *Holiday Reflections Cookbook.* New Braunfels, Texas: Sophienburg Museum and Archives.
Texas State Historical Association, *The Handbook of Texas,* Vol. I, 1952.
"The Diary of Eliza (Mrs. Albert Sidney) Johnston." *Southwestern Quarterly LX 4, 1957.*
Thornton, Mrs. Paul F., and Mrs. W. (I. V.) Davis, comp. *Our Home Cookbook.* Austin, Texas: The First Cumberland Presbyterian Church, 1891.
Washtensaw County Pioneer Society. *Dr. Chase's Recipes – Medicine Book: 30 Home Remedies.* Ann Arbor, Michigan, 1886.
White House Cookbook: . . . 1887.
Woodhull, Frost, "Ranch Remedies." *The Cattleman.* n.d.

Index

Options at Sea 1
Sweet Thick Rice, 3
Meal Pudding (Mehl Pudding), 4
Wein (Wine) Beiguss (Sauce) for
 Pudding, 5
Boiled Pork, 5
White Bread, 6
Lentil Soup, 6
Spaetzle, 8

Beverages 9
Weinsaft (Grape Juice), 9
German Champagne Punch, 9
Cherry Brandy, 10
Currant or Blackberry Wine, 10
Blackberry Cordial, 10
Quince Cordial, 10
How to Make Coffee, 11
Cream Soda Without a Fountain, 11
Aromatic Beer, 12
A Temperance Pledge, 12

Breads 13
Apple Fritters, 13
Baking Powder Biscuit, 13
Hominy Fritters, 14
Corn Meal Mush — Buttered, 14
Crackling Corn Bread, 14
Egg Corn Bread, 14
Narcissa Cothran's Spoon Bread, 15
Doughnuts, 15
Lone Star Doughnuts, 15

All Graham Flour Biscuits, 15
Corn Meal Griddle Cakes, 16
Griddle Cakes, 16
Watermelon Syrup, 16
How to Cook Ranch Griddle
 Cakes, 16
Pearl Donegan's Griddle Pancakes,
 17
Homemade Bread Starter for
 Perpetual Yeast, 17
Hoe Cake, 17
Perpetual Yeast Bread, 18
Cheese Straws, 18
Stollen, 18
Salt Rising Bread, 19
Scotch Short-cake, 19
Johnny Cakes, 20
Pumpkin Bread, 20
Pineapple Nut Bread, 20
Rice Bread, 20
Milk Toast, 21
Corn Bread, 21
Spider Corn Cake, 21
Corn Dodgers, 21
Raised Potato-cake, 22
Egg Biscuit, 22
Sally Lunn, 22
Scotch Scones, 22
Flannel Cakes, 23
Apple Fritters, 23

Crullers, 24
Crackling Bread, 24
Bread, Camp Fire Style, 24
Breakfast Cush, 25
Prepared Flour, 25

Soups 26
Beef Soup with Okra, 26
Corned Beef Soup, 26
Mutton Broth, 27
Black Bean Soup, 27
Tomato Soup, 27
Farm Ox-Tail Soup, 27
Beef Tea, 27
Squirrel Soup, 28
Gumbo or Okra Soup, 29
Force Meat Ball Soup, 29
Fish Soup, 29
Bouillon, 30
Caramel for Soup, 30

Butter, Cheese, and Eggs 31
To Make Butter Quickly, 31
Cottage Cheese, 31
Cheese Souffle, 32
Scalloped Cheese, 32
Cayenne Cheese Straws, 32
Welsh Rarebit, 33
Shirred Eggs, 33
Apple Omelet, 33
Cheese Fondue, 34
Baked Omelet, 34
The Best Egg Custard, 34
Mushroom Omelet, 35
Ham Omelet, 35

Fish 36
Hurricane Oysters, 36
Broiled Shad, 36
Baked Shad, 37
Broiled Salmon, 37
Baked Salmon with Cream Sauce, 37
Salmon Croquettes, 37
Fish Balls, 38
Halibut Cutlets, 38

Fish Fritters, 38
Stewed Terrapin, with Cream, 39
Entree of Shrimps and Tomatoes, 39
To Make a Crab Pie, 39
Roast Clams in the Shell, 40
Frogs Fried, 40

Meat, Poultry, and Game 41
Pioneer Meals on the Trail to
  Texas, 41
Pioneer Style Meat, 41
Cornbread Dressing, 42
Advice for Boiling Meat, 42
Southern Boiled Ham, 42
Grandma's Sugar Cure, 43
Ham Stuffed Peppers, 43
Meat Cure, 43
Son-of-a-Gun Stew, 44
Summer Sausage, 44
Deep Fried Chicken, 44
Christmas Roast Goose, 45
Christmas Season with the 2nd
  Cavalry in Texas, 45
How to Cook Young Chickens, 48
Fried Chicken with Cream Sauce, 49
Chicken Croquettes, 49
Pickled Chicken, 49
Chicken Cheese, 50
Chicken Patties, 50
Broiled Chicken on Toast, 50
Braised Duck, 50
Duck Pie, 51
Stewed Pigeons, 51
Roast Partridges, 52
Pigeon Pie, 52
Broiled Pigeons or Squabs, 52
Squirrel, 52
Broiled Rabbits, 53
Broiled Venison Steak, 53
Venison Hashed, 53
Barb-B-Que Venison, 54
Tamale de Cuscela (Corn Meal Pot
  Pie), 54
Ham Pie, 54

Chili y Huevos con Carne (Pepper and Eggs with Meat), 55
Chili Reyenes (Stuffed Peppers), 55

Sauces and Dressings 56
Drawn Butter, 56
Egg Sauce, or White Sauce, 56
Onion Sauce, 57
Texas Tomato Catsup, 57
Mint Sauce, 57
Sharp Brown Sauce, 57
Wine Sauce for Game, 58
Brandy or Wine Sauce, 58
Currant Jelly Sauce, 58
Cider Apple Sauce, 58
Sauce Piquante, 59
To Dress Curry (Bombay), 59

Dumplings 60
Swedish Dumplings, 60
Sauerkraut and Dumplings, 60
Never Fail Chicken and Dumplings, 61
Apple Dumplings, 61

Salads and Salad Dressings 62
Be Not Wasteful, 62
Lambs Quarter Weed and Kerlis Weed, 62
Southern Ambrosia Salad, 63
Tante Sida's Salad Dressing, 63
Margaret Stiles' Salad Dressing, 63
Mayonnaise Dressing, 64
Dressing for Cold Slaw, 64
Mrs. George Hume's Cream Dressing for Cold Slaw, 65
Salad Dressing for Lettuce, 65
Tuna Salad, 65
Cucumber Salad, 65
Dandelion Salad, 66
Chicken Salad, 66
Mixed Summer Salad, 66
Orange and Banana Salad, 67
Ham Salad, 67

Pimento Salad, 67
Margaret Stiles' Mayonnaise, 67
Potato Salad, Hot, 68

Vegetables and Pasta 69
Spaetzle, 69
Noodles, 70
Texas Okra and Tomatoes, 70
Stuffed Cabbage (Gefullte Kohl), 70
Tomato Bell, 71
Tomatoes and Cream, 71
Baked Beans, 72
Chili Beans, 72
Great Grandmother's Baked Beans, 73
Fried Squash, 73
Boiled Leeks, 73
Carrots and Corn, 74
Sauerkraut, 74
To Cook Rice so that Its Grains Will Stand Alone, 75
Baked Cauliflower, 75
Stewed Celery, 75
Buttered Onions, 75
Fried Okra, 76
Hominy, 76
Potato Puffs, 76
Baked Sweet Potatoes, 76
A Good Recipe for Poor Sweet Potatoes, 76
Oysterettes, 77
Onions Baked, 77
Fried Cucumbers, 77
Corn Pudding, 77
Fried Egg-Plant, 78
Chop Suey, 78

Cakes 79
Wedding Cake, 79
Chocolate Potato Cake, 80
Deluxe Chocolate Fudge Frosting, 81
Kate Hurt's Potato Cake, 81
Oma Streuer's Nuss Torte (Nut Cake), 81

Powdered Sugar Icing for Nuss Torte, 82
Chocolate Butter Frosting, 82
Poor Man's Cake, 82
Mama's Ground Pecan Cake, 82
The Goblet Cake, 83
Feather Cake, 83
Cake of 1846, 84
Great-Grandmother Kincaid's Favorite White Cake, 84
Great-Grandmother's Marble Cake, 84
Pound Cake, 85
Black Angel Cake, 85
Yellow Angel Food Cake, 86
A Pioneer Birthday Cake, 86
Taylor Cake, 87
Old Timey Stack Cake, 87
Coconut Cake, 87
Prune Cake, 88
Eggless Spice Cake, 88
Granny Golden's Spice Cake, 89
Nut and Date Filling, 89
Hot Milk Cake, 89
Loaf or Layer Cake, 90
Economy, 90
Poverty Cake, 90
Carrot Cake, 91
Gingerbbread with Chocolate Glaze, 91
Banana Cake, 91
Geranium Cake, 92
Baking Advice, 92
Lemon Queen Cake, 92
White Fruit Cake, 92
Old Fashioned Ginger Cake or Bread, 93
Pork Cake, Without Butter, Milk, or Eggs, 93
1900 Bride Cake, 94
Frosting Without Eggs, 95
Cream Filling for Layer Cake, 95
Rose Coloring for Frosting, Jellies, Ice Cream, Etc., 95
Three Egg Bake, 95
"Filling," 95

Cookies 96
Old Fashion Molasses Cookes, 96
Sorgum Ginger Bread, 96
Orange Cookies, 97
Great-Grandmother Tenery's Oatmeal Cookies, 97
Pecan Macaroons, 97
Edna's Ice Box Cookies, 98
Pfeffernusse (Peppernuts), 98
Pecan Praline Cookies, 99
Lebkuchen, 99
Oatmeal Rocks, 100
Cinnamon Stars, 100
Rough and Ready Cake, 101
Tea Cakes, 102
Berry Tea Cakes, 102

Puddings 103
Saving, 103
Rice Blanc Mange, 103
Sweet Potato Pudding, 104
Woodford Pudding, 104
Date Pudding, 104
Apple Float, 105
Edna Rogers Alexander's Bread Pudding, 105
Tapioca Pudding, 105
Italian Snow, 105
Floating Island, 106
Orioles Nest, 106
Breaded Tomato Pudding, 106
English Plum Pudding, 107
Sauce for Plum Pudding, 107
Baked Corn Meal Pudding, 107
Delicate Indian Pudding, 107
Cottage Pudding, 108
Rose Brandy, 108

Pastry, Pies, and Tarts **109**
The Art of Cooking, 109
Deep Fried Apple Pies, 109
Green Grape Pie, 110
Sweet Potato Pie, 110
Pumpkin Pie, 111
Pearl Donna's Pecan Pie, 111
Texas Buttermilk Pie, 111
Old, Old Pie Crust Recipe, 112
Green Grape Cobbler, 112
Apple Custard Pie, 113
Apple and Peach Meringue Pie, 113
Lemon Custard Pie, 113
Lemon Pie, 113
Mrs. Conley's Lemon Pie, 114
Jelly Pies, 114
Margaret Youngblood Stiles' Pecan Pie, 115
Custard Pie, 115
Green Tomato Pie, 115
Grape Pie, 116
Mince Meat for Pies, 116
Ripe Berry Pie, 116
Peach Pie, 117
Stewed Pumpkin or Squash for Pies, 117
Pumpkin Pie, 117
Osgood Pies, 118
Mrs. Ten Evck's Molasses Pie, 118
Fine Puff Pastry, 118
Rules for Under Crust, 119
Strawberry Tartlets, 119
Tarts, 119
Fruit Turnovers, 120
Orange Tartlets, 120
Maids of Honor, 120
Apple Tarts, 121
Blackberry Cobbler, 121

Custards, Creams, and Desserts for Levees and Other Occasions **122**
A Levee at the President of the Republic of Texas' House, 122
Soft Caramel Custard, 123
Cup Custard, 123
Apple Custard, 123
Charlotte Russe, 124
Whipped Cream, 124
Bavarian Cream, 124
Gelatine Jelly Without Boiling, 125
Peach Cream, 125
Orange Trifle, 125
Fruit Trifle, 125
Moonshine, 126
Sponge Cake, 126
Cake and Sauce for Dinner, 126
Laura Driskill's Moonshine, 127
Floating Island, 127
Fruit Blanc Mange, 127
Spanish Cream, 127
Huevos Reales (Royal Eggs), 128
Copa Mexicanas, 128
Strawberry Charlotte, 128
Tipsy Charlotte, 129
Dessert Puffs, 129
Stewed Apples, 129
Chocolate Macroons, 130
Ice Cream, 130
Chocolate Ice Cream, 130
Custard Ice Cream, 130
Raspberry Sherbert, 131
To Have a Happy Life, 131

Candy **132**
Chocolate Caramels, 132
Divinity Fudge, 132
Sugarplums, 132
Fruit Fudge, 133
Butterscotch Candy, 133
Christmas Pudding Candy, 134
Chewy Candy, 134
Chewy Mexican Pecan Pralines, 135
Mexican Candy, 135
Divinity, 135
Chocolate Drops, 136
Fondant for Candy, 136
Peppermint Drops, 136

Molasses Candy, 137
Crystallized Rose Petals, 137
Cream Peanuts, 137
Peanut Pralines, 138
Date Loaf, 138
Date Loaf Candy, 138
Action of Sugar or Candy on the
   Teeth, 139

Canning and Pickling 140
Corn Salat, 140
Sweet Pickled Cucumber Rings, 140
Ochra and Tomatoes, 141
Tomato Paste, 141
Green Tomato Catsup, 141
Cucumber Catsup, 142
Apple Catsup, 142
Green Tomato Pickles (Sweet), 142
Pickled Cabbage, 143
Pepper Mangoes, 143
Pickled Onions, 143
Chow Chow, 144
Chow Chow, 144
Pickled Beets, 145
An Ornamental Pickle, 145
Mixed Pickles, 145
Chopped Pickles, 145
Yellow Pickle, 146
Spiced Plums, 146
Peach or Plum Sweet Pickles, 146
Sweet Pickle Peaches, 147
Spiced Peaches, 147

Household Hints 148
Decorations for a Party During the
   Republic of Texas, 148
TOILET RECIPES
   Rose Water, 149
   Jockey Club Bouquet, 149
   Lavender Water, 149
   Cream of Roses, 149
   Cream of Lilies, 149
   Powder for the Face, 149
   Lip Salve, 150

Oxmarrow-Pomade for the Hair,
   150
To Increase the Hair in the
   Brows, 150
Cold Cream, 150
Hair Dye, 150
Hair Wash, 151
To Remove Freckles, 151
To Remove Moth Patches, 151
Tooth Powder, 151
Bad Breath, 152
Razor-Strop Paste, 152
Bandoline, 152
CARE OF CLOTHING
   To Clean Black Lace, No. 1, 152
   To Clean Black Lace, No. 2, 153
   To Remove Paint from Black
      Silk, 153
   To Wash White Thread Lace,
      153
   Novel Dress Mending, 153
   Polish or Enamel for Shirtwaists,
      153
   To Dye Straw Bonnets Brown, 154
   Clothes that have a Bad Odor, 154
SCHOOL AND HOME AIDS
   Glue and Cement, 154
   Paste, 155
   To Make Tracing Paper, 155
CREEPY CRAWLY THINGS
   Troublesome Ants, 155
   Cockroaches Destroyed, 155
   Fleas, 156
HOUSEHOLD MAINTENANCE
   An Erasive Fluid for the
      Removal of Spots on Furniture
      or Fabrics Without Injuring
      the Color, 156
   To Ventilate a Room, 156
   Tallow Candles for Summer
      Use, 156
   An Agreeable Disinfectant, 157

To Mend Sheets, 157
To Prevent Creaking of Bedsteads, 157
Creaking Hinge's Prevented, 157
Lead Pipes, 157
To Pick up Broken Glass, 157
Care of Kitchen Sink, 158
To Wash Dishes, 158
Removal of Grease from Floor, 158
To Clean Furniture, 158
Food Keeper, 158
To Clean Carpets and Rugs, 159
Cheap Carpet, 159
Make Rag Rugs, 159
To Lay a Carpet, 159
Stair Carpets, 160
To Make Garden Walks, 160
To Destroy Weeds in Walks, 160
To Mend Tin, 160
Cess Pools Disinfected Instantly, 160
To Temper Lamp Chimneys, 161
Magic Furniture Polish, 161

TO LIGHTEN THE WASHING CHORES
Spots from Wash Goods, 161
To Remove Ink, Wine, or Fruit Stains, 161
To Set Colors in Washable Clothes, 161
The Weekly Wash, 161
Home Made Lye Soap, 163
To Retain Colors, 163
Bleaching Clothes, 163
To Prevent Rust on Flat Irons, 163

CHILD CARE AND GAMES
Infant Care, 163
Queen Anne and Her Maids, 164
Buzz, 165
How to be Happy Tho Married, 166

Home Remedies 168
To Keep the Feet Dry, 168
Cerate of Spanish Fly, 168
Cure for Pimples, 169
To Stop Hiccups, 169
Stye, 169
Ringworm, 169
Red Bug Bites, 170
Spider Bites, 170
Chiggers, 170
Ant Bite, 170
Cuts or Puncture Wounds, 170
Laxative, 170
Bladder and Kidney Trouble, 171
Kidney Trouble, 171
Liver Remedy, 171
Sores, 171
Colds and Fever, 171
Fevers, 172
Ague, Chills and Fever, 172
Asthma, 172
Birthmarks, 172
Bleeding, 172
Bunions, 173
Ringworm, 173
Rheumatism, 173
Chapped Hands, 173
Colds, 173
Dropsy, 173
Bone Felons, 174
Arrow Wounds, 174
Lockjaw, 174
Gun Shot Wounds, 174
Lunacy, 174
Lung Trouble, 174
Pneumonia, 174
Skunk Bites, 175
Sore Throat, 175
Teething Babies, 175
First Aid Outfit, 175
Graefenberg Vegetable Pills, 176
Pile Ointment, 177

For Stiff Joints, 177
Dropsy Receipt, 178

Conversion Charts 179
Conversions from Then to Now, 179
Weights and Measures, 179
Baking, 180
Tables of Weights and
 Measures, 180
Measurements, 180
Substitutions, 181

Translations 182

Contributors 183
Reuben Hornsby Chapter
 (Austin), 183
Stephen F. Austin Chapter
 (Austin), 184
Texian Chapter (Austin), 185
William Barret Travis Chapter
 (Austin), 186
Baron de Bastrop Chapter
 (Bastrop), 188

Dr. Wilhelm Keidel Chapter
 (Fredericksburg), 189
Gonzales Chapter (Gonzales), 190
Monument Hill Chapter (La
 Grange), 191
Oran Milo Roberts Chapter
 (Lampasas), 192
Llano Chapter (Llano), 193
Cornelius Smith Chapter
 (Luling), 194
Ferdinand Lindheimer Chapter
 (New Braunfels), 195
Martin Wells Chapter (Round
 Rock), 197
Moon McGehee Chapter (San
 Marcos), 198
Abishai Mercer Dickson Chapter
 (Seguin), 199
Elizabeth Zumwalt Kent Chapter
 (Smiley), 200

Bibliography (Partial) 201

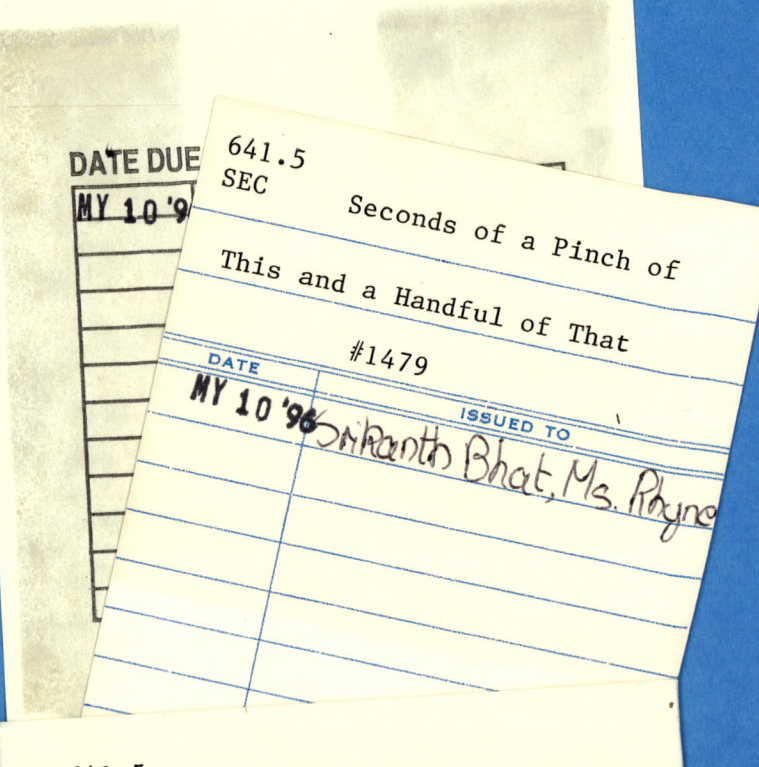

641.5
SEC   Seconds of a Pinch of
This and a Handful of That
#1479

DATE DUE
MY 10 '96

ISSUED TO
Srikanth Bhat, Ms. Rhyne

641.5
SEC   Seconds of a Pinch of This and
       a Handful of That

GRADY MIDDLE SCHOOL LIBRARY